GOD'S FIDELITY TO US

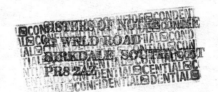

Brian McNeil

God's fidelity to us

Biblical reflections
on the God who calls

ST PAULS

Cover illustration by Alessandro Nastasio, used by courtesy of Edizioni San Paolo, s.r.l., Italy

ST PAULS
Middlegreen, Slough SL3 6BT, United Kingdom
Moyglare Road, Maynooth, Co. Kildare, Ireland

© ST PAULS (UK)
ISBN 085439 512 1
Printed by Biddles Ltd, Guildford

ST PAULS is an activity of the priests and brothers of the Society of St Paul who proclaim the Gospel through the media of social communication

To
John C. O'Neill
on his sixty-fifth birthday

"It is the Lord who goes before you;
he will be with you,
he will not fail you or forsake you;
do not fear or be dismayed."
(Deut 31:8)

Contents

Part I: IN THE OLD COVENANT

I	Salvation history: my history	11
II	God calls Abram	21
III	A new name	27
IV	The sacrifice of Abraham	37
V	The call of Moses	47
VI	Jeremiah's call	61
VII	His strength in our weakness	75

Part II: IN THE NEW COVENANT

VIII	God calls Mary	85
IX	The visitation	95
X	Under the Cross	107
XI	Joseph's vocation	117
XII	Not servants but friends	125
XIII	Peter: vocation and forgiveness	143
XIV	Conclusion	153

Part I

IN THE OLD COVENANT

I
Salvation history: my history

Some years ago, when the parish priest of a town near our monastery was dying of cancer, the Bishop asked my Abbot if I could take over the parish as administrator for a short period. This meant seven months of intense and very enjoyable pastoral activity in a parish of 9,500 people about twenty miles outside Rome. The priest whom I replaced had been seriously ill for some time, and I found that the fundamental sustaining force of pastoral life was five groups of the Neo-Catechumenate. Without them, the parish could have closed its doors long before I came. They gave the catechesis in preparation for the sacraments of baptism, first communion, confirmation and marriage, and they found priests who could celebrate Mass at the weekends. One of my main activities was the celebration of a liturgy of the word for each of these groups in turn. This involved discussions of biblical texts, which were introduced by a member of the community in the course of the liturgy.

The Neo-Catechumenate, like the other "ecclesial movements" that have spread in the years after Vatican II, has been the object of a great deal of criticism. The commonest accusation levelled against them is that they are proclaiming and living out an elitist version of Christianity. I do not want to discuss these questions here, because whatever may be the case with this or other movements as a whole, I myself learned one fundamental thing from the groups in my parish. As I listened to the groups speaking of biblical passages, I was repeatedly struck by the phrase they used: "la mia storia", "my history". For them, the events of the Bible were not *other people's history*, in a far-off time and place, in a culture and mentality tremendously distant from their own: in the texts they read, they discerned their own history. In the story of Israel's deliverance from slavery in Egypt, they discerned the story of their own deliverance from sin and death; the crossing of the Red Sea was the story of their own baptism. The teaching of St Paul was addressed, not primarily to hearers long dead, but to them today.

There is nothing new in such an interpretation, of course: it is absolutely typical of the Church's tradition as this is expressed in the eastern and western fathers and liturgies. For example, after Ex 14 has been read in the Easter Vigil, we pray: "Lord God, in the new covenant you shed light on the miracles you worked in ancient times: the Red Sea is a symbol of our baptism, and the nation you freed from slavery is a sign of your Christian people..." But what is new, in my experience, is that people who have no first-hand knowledge of the church fathers simply discover for themselves the coherence between "salvation history" and "my history". The primary question then is not: "What did the text mean for them then?", although this is obviously very important, but: "What does the text mean for us to-day?"

Everything that follows in this book is based on the insight that salvation history is *my history*, that the God who revealed himself in the past in the manner scripture narrates is the God who reveals himself to me today in the same manner. The Holy Spirit, who makes the written word come alive today in the Church, does not limit his activity to ensuring that the Pope and the bishops interpret the Bible correctly. He is at work in me, as I hear and read the Bible, in such a way that this word is addressed to me personally, here, within the fellowship of the Church today. This personal word is spoken to me and is both *an encounter with God* and *a mission,* as we see in some of the great "vocational" stories of Church history.

– In his biography of St Antony the Great (+ 356), St Athanasius relates how Antony, then aged about twenty, went into the village church one day and heard the words of Matthew's Gospel: "If you wish to be perfect, go, sell what you possess and give it to the poor, and you will have a treasure in heaven. Then come and follow me!" (19:21). This was certainly not the first time that Antony had heard these words. But now he realised that they were being spoken *to him*, that *he* was the rich young man of the story and that *he* had to do what Jesus commanded. He left the church "immediately", says Athanasius, and did what the Gospel text said. Thanks to the immense popularity of Athanasius' work, this story became classical. But it is by no means unique, as another example from the beginning of the fifth century shows.

– Theodoret of Cyrrhus, relating the vocation of St Simeon the Stylite (+ 459), tells how he went to the village church with his parents and heard the Beatitudes read (Mt 5:5ff). The words, "Blessed are the mourners", struck him so deeply that he took up the solitary life, and later climbed his famous pillar. In order to receive the blessings promised *to him* personally by Jesus, he adopted the form of life that he judged best suited to make *him* a "mourner".

– A similar kind of discovery takes place when St Thérèse of Lisieux (+ 1897) reads St Paul's words on love in 1 Cor 13 and realises that this is *her own* vocation; and when Blessed Elizabeth of the Trinity (+ 1906) reads Eph 1 and discovers *her own* vocation when Paul says that we are called to be "a praise of the glory" of God, *laudem gloriae*. These were not texts previously unknown to the nuns: they were texts that became lit up by the Holy Spirit in such a way that they became "my history" for them.

It is important to note that each of these four personal discoveries of an individual vocation involves a relationship to the Church. Antony and Simeon sought the solitary life, and Thérèse and Elizabeth were already enclosed

Carmelites; but the discovery of their intensely personal and individual path paradoxically "displaced" them, pushing them *outwards*. Antony and Simeon became fathers of communities of monks; indeed, Simeon on his pillar drew the crowds from all over the world in an even more dramatic and public fashion than the stigmatised Capuchin Padre Pio in San Giovanni Rotondo in the fifty years before his death in 1968. Their fatherhood continued after their deaths. Antony is the father of all monks everywhere, but there is an even more literal and geographical sense in which we can say that his children are still to be found: the last twenty-five years have seen an immense renewal of monastic life in the Egyptian desert, under the guidance of figures like Father Matta el Meskin. There are (as far as I know) no stylites left today, but Simeon ignited a tradition that lasted until well into the nineteenth century, when the last stylite died in Russia. Thérèse and Elizabeth have exercised a motherhood over millions of believers through their writings.

Thus these charisms, discovered in the intensely personal discovery each made of "*my history*" in the written Word of God, were given, not for the sake of the four saints as individuals, but for the sake of their brothers and sisters.

In the biblical meditations in this book, we shall constantly look for the elements in the story which make "salvation history" become "my history". The perspective is that of "the God who calls" – as we traditionally say, the perspective of "vocation". I have drawn on many examples from Church history and from my own experience to illustrate what I want to say, and both these factors mean that religious life and the priesthood feature very prominently. But this is not meant to exclude those who are neither religious nor priests. There is in fact only one Christian vocation, because God calls us all to only one path: to follow his Son and be configured to him. This is what the Second Vatican Council meant by speaking of the universal call to holiness. Thus any authentic Christian experience of the God who calls has something significant to communicate to all other authentic Christian experiences of the God who calls. The principle of finding "my history" in the biblical narratives can be applied to all forms and situations of the Christian response to the one Lord.

* * *

I conclude this introductory chapter with a brief meditation on a story from John's Gospel which illustrates fundamental themes of this book: the encounter between Jesus and Mary Magdalene on Easter morning (20:14ff).

The first point we note is that, although we can say that Mary Magdalene loves Jesus and that this is the reason why she comes to his grave "early on the first day of the week, while it was still dark", this is a love for someone who is *dead*. It is a grief unmitigated by any hope of actually meeting Jesus. If Mary believed in a resurrection, this would have been only in the terms Martha uses of her brother Lazarus, "I know that he will rise again in the resurrection at the last day" (11:24). No, for Mary Jesus is dead and buried – there can be no encounter between the living and the dead. She comes only to weep.

When she does see Jesus, she thinks he is the gardener. He stands before her, but for her, this is a wholly impersonal meeting; he addresses her with a general title: "Woman, why are you weeping?", and she replies equally impersonally: "Sir, if it was you who took him away..." If this meeting is to be converted into a personal encounter, the initiative can come only from Jesus, who now addresses her by name: "Mary!" And now she addresses him with a title which expresses the relationship of a believing disciple to the Master: "Rabbuni!" On the far side of the death which had terminated the old relationship between Jesus and Mary Magdalene, *he calls her by name* and offers her an utterly new relationship as his gift in response to her love – a gift that immeasurably exceeds anything that might be "owed" to her for the love that had brought her out to his grave early in the morning.

* * *

But as soon as Mary accepts this new relationship of love, the Master *sends her out*: "Do not cling to me... but *go to my brothers* and say to them, 'I am ascending to my Father and your Father, to my God and your God'." This new paschal relationship with Jesus is not to be a private spiritual possession of Mary Magdalene. The encounter with Jesus is at the same time a mission: she is to go to the disciples and assure them that they are the "brothers" of Jesus. His Father is now likewise their Father, his God is now likewise their God. And so she proclaims: "I have seen the Lord."

The initiative lies with the one who calls, not with the one who is called. As Jesus says in his farewell discourse, "It was not *you* who chose me: rather, *I* chose you and appointed you to go and bear fruit" (Jn 15:16). The ground can indeed be prepared to receive the seed of the divine call – as Mary's ground is prepared through her love for Jesus, or the rich young man's ground through the observance of all the commandments ("All this I have kept; what do I still lack?", Mt 19:20). But the call, the vocation which the Lord offers, is utterly out of proportion to anything the person called can offer to the Lord. Mary Magdalene did not expect to meet Jesus in the garden and be sent to proclaim his resurrection; far less did she "deserve" such a call. Likewise, the rich young man neither expected nor deserved Jesus' invitation to abandon his wealth and follow him. In each case, the initiative lies absolutely with the Lord.

The call always comes as an invitation. God respects our freedom, which is his own gift to us. No one is ever compelled to believe, and no one is ever constrained by divine force to accept a vocation against his own free choice. Jesus' call, "Mary!", is an invitation to her to accept a new relationship to him and a mission to his "brothers". If she had refused this invitation, salvation history would have had to be written differently. But she would never have been coerced into a ministry that she herself did not wish to carry out.

The following chapters will develop these brief points by meditating on other biblical figures. But a final point, picking up what I said at the beginning of this chapter about *la mia storia*, is particularly relevant both to Mary Magdalene and to ourselves.

When she comes to the disciples, she proclaims that Jesus has risen *by speaking about her own history*: "I have seen the Lord!" This is not an autobiographical statement, in the modern sense of that word. Rather, like Nehemiah's story of his own life in the Old Testament, it is a testimony to the greatness of God fashioned from the elements of Mary's own history. We cannot delete her from her own proclamation, any more than we can delete Paul from his proclamation ("Have I not seen Jesus our Lord?", 1 Cor 9:1), as if we should thereby get at the "essential" dogma hidden behind the personal anecdote. The history of Mary and Paul *is* the proclamation of the resurrection. The Lord whom they proclaim by telling their own history is not an abstract theological idea, but one who has acted in their own lives.

I may or may not be able to identify one single event in my life as the decisive encounter with the Lord in which I received my individual vocation to serve him and his brothers and sisters; often, we look back on a long process of searching and slow clarification, rather than to one specific date in the calendar. But whatever my history may have been, it forms an essential element of my testimony. I myself in the concrete events of my life am a part of my message about the Lord, and I cannot delete this part in order to get at some supposedly "essential" event. Without the history, without the anchoring of my proclamation in *events*, my words can never be more than the communication of an idea. That, of course, is a pretty safe kind of proclamation – it is much more risky to say, with Mary Magdalene, "I have seen the Lord". But if the word of God is not incarnate in "my history", then he will not save the genuine person that I am in my concrete historical existence. At most, he will save the world of my ideas.

It is easy to object to what I have just written by pointing out how dangerous "experience" can be as a criterion in theology (for example, in claimed mystical experiences and private revelations) and by insisting that experience has to be checked over against the objectivity of the Church's magisterium. This point is perfectly correct. Just as Mary Magdalene's experience sent her "to my brothers" with her testimony, so we too are always sent "to my brothers", i.e. to the Church, with our testimony to what God has done in our history. Vocation (in every sense of the word) has to be affirmed within the Church, and that inevitably means affirmation at some level of the hierarchical structures which are God's gift to his Church. My point, however, is quite different and must not be misunderstood: if the proclamation which I make is not anchored anywhere within my individual history, so that I am not in fact able to say that "I have seen the Lord", then I have disincarnated the Word and neutralised God's power to *act*.

The reasons for falling numbers of vocations to religious life and to the diocesan priesthood are complex and numerous. Some of them, such as the reduced "pool" of potential candidates caused by the reduced birth rate, are certainly not the fault of priests and religious themselves! But part of the reason may be our failure of nerve, our fear of identifying our own lives as the place where God has shown himself and acted to save us. Speaking of vocations, Pope John Paul II has noted that "Life generates life". "Life" comes from the deeply personal encounter with Jesus Christ as the Lord who calls me to himself and sends me out to his brothers and sisters. If we can find the courage to speak of this encounter and so to let others share in our experience (not merely in our theological ideas or pastoral strategies), then our "life" may generate "life" in others, who will likewise be able to say, "I have seen the Lord".

II
God calls Abram

Salvation history begins in Genesis with a divine call, a vocation. After the long downward trend in the first eleven chapters of Genesis, symbolised in the steadily decreasing lifespans in the genealogies and culminating in the confusion of human languages at Babel, it is God himself who intervenes to change the course of events. The initiative comes from God alone: nothing has happened since the days of the flood to alter the situation that "the wickedness of humankind was great in the earth, and every inclination of the thoughts of their hearts was only evil continually" (Gen 6:5). God breaks into this hopeless situation by *speaking*: "The Lord said to Abram..." (12:1).

This is no silent God, no creator who merely "sets the ball rolling" and then withdraws to let his creation get on with things. This is a God who acts, and more specifically a God who speaks. Speaking is a sign of love. Love impels us to communicate with one another, and where we stop speaking to each other, love will not long endure. God speaks to Abram because he loves him – and in loving Abram and calling this one man, he expresses his love for us all.

"Go from your country and your kindred and your father's house to the land that I will show you. I will make of you a great nation, and I will bless you, and make your name great, so that you will be a blessing. I will bless those who bless you, and the one who curses you I will curse; and in you all the families of the earth shall be blessed."

These words contain both a demand and a promise.

* * *

God demands a threefold uprooting: "from your country and your kindred and your father's house". "Uprooting" is not too strong a word, for this demand goes to the very roots of what makes Abram the person he is. He is already seventy-five years old (12:4), and thus is no longer in the position of a young man leaving his home to establish himself in life (like the prodigal son in Jesus' parable, Lk 15). He is already rich, with many possessions and servants; obviously, he is someone who counts in his own society, and he is able to impress himself on those whom he encounters in the lands he comes to, and to take an important part in their local wars (cf. chapters 14 and 23). "Your country" is, we may presume, not only the country to which Abram belongs, but also the country that belongs to Abram. He must also give up his family ties, taking with him only his wife Sarai and his nephew Lot. He must uproot himself from all that is familiar to him, from the people of his father's house and all the net of social relationships which constitute "his" world. A person's identity is not independent of all these factors: I am who I am, precisely because I can locate myself in reference to all this. God's call means a radical dislocation and expropriation.

He must leave what is known and journey into what is unknown. This is a fundamental characteristic of every vocation: whether or not an actual geographical departure is involved (as for example in the case of missionaries), there is always some kind of uprooting, some kind of renunciation of what is known for the sake of what is unknown. I must leave everything that is "mine", country and kindred and father's house, if not physically and materially, then at least in the sense that "my" world is no longer to be constituted by these factors alone: I set my sights on the radically new land of God's promise.

The only path to the promise is the path of uprooting.

And this path is always painful, if it is taken seriously – that is to say, without compromise and without a safety-net. "Go," says God, implying a radical break with Abram's present situation as a wealthy, respected elderly man. The religious life has been understood from ancient times as the following of Abram: like him, we hear the call of God to depart from our country, our kindred and our father's house. The pain involved for a young person today is not the same pain of uprooting for someone already established in life like Abram, but there are important similarities.

Abram is called within a society that is not primarily concerned to regulate its life in terms of the word of Yahweh. His obedience to Yahweh's call was not, therefore, an act that made sense to his fellow citizens in Haran. It was not something that fitted into their notions of a *normal* response to the divine. A young person called today to the uprooting involved in the religious life or the diocesan priesthood is likewise called within a society which, while not actually hostile to God, runs its life effectively without him. One need only spend a morning reading the daily papers, or an evening watching television, to see a frame of reference that excludes God as irrelevant to "real life": the values assumed to be relevant to the choices we make and to the goals we pursue are wholly innerworldly. Adhesion to the values of one's fellow citizens provides a sense of security, reinforced by approval when one is successful in terms of those values. To enter a novitiate or a seminary today is to take a step that is seen as deeply *abnormal,* a step that proclaims adhesion to other values. If society reacted by persecuting those who took such a step – as was the case in communist eastern Europe, for example – then that reaction would certainly have the effect of reinforcing the conviction of the novices and seminarians that what they were doing was worthwhile; but the duller reality of our pluralist societies is that no one is likely to be challenged by the step we are taking. It will be seen merely as an irrelevance. And those who opt for such an "irrelevance" are truly opting for the unknown, for an extremely difficult life that lacks either support or contestation – either of which would be a help!

The temptation to give up has always existed; Jesus refers to it when he speaks of the one who "puts his hand to the plough and then looks back" (Lk 9:62). The path of uprooting in response to God's call has never been easy, for it involves a death to self in quite specific forms (such as celibacy and obedience) that are very costly. But if the temptation to give up is so especially prominent today as my own experience of religious houses and seminaries suggests, this is surely because of the acute experience of insecurity and genuine *rootlessness in society* experienced by the young people who answer God's call today. Those who work in the formation of candidates, those involved in the apostolate of vocations, and indeed all who have a responsibility for newly-ordained or newly-professed persons, must strive to impart the awareness that those whom God calls are indeed rooted – in him and in his promise. And those who perceive the disharmony between the values of their society and the values of their call, at whatever stage of their lives this happens, must look for stability and rootedness in the same place: in God and in his promise.

* * *

Because the uprooting demanded by God is total, he can offer Abram a promise that embraces the totality of his life. Were God to require less, his promise would have to be correspondingly smaller.

Abram renounces his own land, and God promises him something that goes far beyond any recompense Abram might be thought to have merited for this action: on his arrival in Canaan, "the Lord appeared to Abram, and said, 'To your offspring I will give this land'" (Gen 12:7). Not only is he promised a land in exchange for the land he had left behind: the childless Abram is promised descendants, something that was extremely important in a period with no belief in personal survival of death. We shall see in the following chapters how central this promise was for Abram's history, and how significant it is for ours.

Second, God promises that Abram will "be a blessing... in you all the families of the earth shall be blessed" (12:3). Abram's call is not a purely private affair concerning him alone: his calling will bring a blessing to "all the families of the earth". The personal dimension of the vocation – the call addressed to one man in his individual and unrepeatable circumstances – opens out on to a universal dimension. The two dimensions are inextricably present in this event, just as they are inextricably present in every calling. Even if God calls a person to be a hermit with no physical contact with other people, the person thus called will be "a blessing" for "*all* the families of the earth" precisely by following the individual path indicated by the Lord.

Third, God promises to protect Abram: "I will bless those who bless you, and the one who curses you I will curse." As he says in a later vision, "Do not be afraid, Abram, I am your shield" (15:1). The God who manifests himself to Abram is a God who makes radical demands of him, but who does not abandon him. He will reward Abram's friends and fight against Abram's enemies. In other words, God *commits himself* to Abram. The covenant entails obligations on God, not only obligations on his human partner.

Here again is an absolutely fundamental principle of the Christian life: "I am your shield." What counts in the struggles of following Christ is never my strength or my fidelity, but the strength and the fidelity of the God who has committed himself to me by calling me to serve him. His call to me obliges him to protect me. No strength – whether the external strength of persecution or the internal strength of temptation – no matter how powerful or even overwhelming it may be when measured in human terms, can ever be stronger than God's strength. God does not promise Abram an easy passage, but he does promise him divine protection. He does not promise us that our path will be smooth and our progress steady, he gives us no guarantee that the negative powers will be neutralised: but he does promise us his protection. If we build our house on the rock of his promise, our house will not fall. If, of course, we prefer to build on the sand of our own fidelity and strength, then sooner or later the storms will sweep our house away.

This promise of protection extends to the whole of our lives, a promise that no trials will ever be too powerful for us. God gives us no guarantees that the trials will be brief; they can involve repeated experiences of deep emotional suffering, doubts about faith, devastating loneliness, uncertainty about whether one did choose the right path after all, the torment of sexual longing. Our greatest trial may quite simply be our own personality itself – learning to live with oneself and to love oneself can take a whole lifetime. God's promise is that he will be our "shield" in all such trials. They will never be so great that we *must* give up in face of them. He will bring us out into the open, on the other side of them.

The reasons why some people do give up their commitment to religious life, or marriage, or the priesthood, are complex and individual. They resist generalisation, and the individuals involved should not be condemned or ostracised within the Church. What can be said to those fighting against the difficulties is that the God who has called them is faithful and that he is indeed their "shield". If they take the risk of trusting themselves to him (perhaps only in the words of the young desert monk in his temptations: "Lord, save me, whether I want you to or not!"), then they will *experience* his fidelity.

For it is ultimately a question of experience, not of a theory about God. It is a question of "my history", in which God manifests the truthfulness of his promise. And this we see in salvation history, in the narrative of God's dealings with Abram, who receives a new name and a son.

III
A new name

When the Lord tells Abram, "Do not be afraid, I am your shield", Abram's reply queries the seriousness of God's words: "O Lord God, what will you give me, for I continue childless, and the heir of my house is Eliezer of Damascus? You have given me no offspring, and so a slave born in my house is to be my heir" (Gen 15:2f). The point is obvious. God had promised Abram, "I will make of you a great nation... To your offspring I will give this land" (12:2,7), but his childlessness gives the lie to God's magnificent promise. The Lord tells him that his slave Eliezer is not to inherit: "Your very own issue shall be your heir" (15:4), and the covenant between Abram and God is solemnly reaffirmed. Yet we read, a few verses later, the sober words, "Now Sarai, Abram's wife, bore him no children" (16:1). What was to be done?

The solution Sarai found was in a legal device whereby the children of a slave-woman counted as the children of her mistress. (The same device is used by the childless Rachel later in the Book of Genesis, specifying that the slave-woman "may bear upon my knees and that I too may have children through her": cf. 30:1ff.) Sarai tells Abram: "Go in to my slave-girl; it may be that I shall obtain children by her" (16:2). And so a son is born to Abram, who is by now eighty-six years old: Ishmael.

This certainly seems to be the fulfilment of God's promises to Abram, who then says to the Lord, "O that Ishmael might live in your sight!" (17:18). But God's plans are not to be executed by human reasoning, as though he were unable to execute them himself. For God is greater than human reasoning. Ishmael is not rejected as a person: "I will bless him and make him fruitful and exceedingly numerous; he shall be the father of twelve princes, and I will make him a great nation" (17:20). But he has no role whatsoever in the salvation history that is *God's initiative*: he is merely the fruit of human reasoning, the fruit of a human attempt to do God's work for him. But only God can keep God's promises, and this he does in a way that goes utterly beyond anything accessible to human reasoning. Abram had believed God's word that his descendants should be as many as the stars of heaven (cf. 15:5f), and so the Lord tells him that it is Sarai his wife who will bear him the son of the promise.

To mark this new phase in salvation history, God bestows on Abram and on Sarai new names: "Abraham", meaning "father of a multitude", and "Sarah", meaning "lady". The promises in chapter 17 are parallel: "No longer shall your name be Abram, but your name shall be Abraham; for I have made you the ancestor of a multitude of nations. I will make you exceedingly fruitful; and I will make nations of you, and kings shall come from you... As for Sarah your wife, you shall not call her Sarai, but Sarah shall be her name. I will bless her, and moreover I will give you a son by her. I will bless her, and she shall give rise to nations; kings of peoples shall come from her." The divine "I" is very important here: the new names are given by God to signify what *he* will do in Abraham and Sarah. This point is underlined by the human reaction: "Then Abraham fell on his face and laughed, and said to himself, 'Can a child be born to a man who is a hundred years old? Can Sarah, who is ninety years old, bear a child?'" It is at this point that human rationality – and common sense – break in: "And Abraham said to God, 'O that Ishmael might live in your sight'" (It is as if he had said, rather less reverently, "Okay, you have had your joke, now let's get back to real life".) But God corrects human rationality and common sense: "No, but your wife Sarah shall bear you a son, and you shall name him Isaac" (i.e., "he laughs"); "my covenant I will establish with Isaac, whom Sarah shall bear to you at this season next year."

It is simply not possible for a woman ninety-year-old to bear a child, and Sarah herself laughs when she hears the prophecy: "After I have grown old, and my husband is old, shall I have pleasure?" (18:12). When Sarah realises that the Lord has overheard her, she "denied, saying, 'I did not laugh'; for she was afraid". But humanly speaking, she had every reason to laugh at such a crazy notion. And yet, despite everything, "The Lord dealt with Sarah as he had said, and the Lord did for Sarah as he had promised. Sarah conceived and bore Abraham a son in his old age, at the time of which God had spoken to him" (21:1f). Note the threefold reference to God's activity in these verses: the human characters play their roles, but the real protagonist of the story is God, acting in their history to fulfil his word and prove his faithfulness. Sarah acknowledges this: "Who would ever have said to Abraham that Sarah would nurse children? Yet I have borne him a son in his old age" (21:7).

If our reaction to this story is the historical question, "Did it actually happen as Genesis says?", we shall doubtless reject it as grotesque, or even tasteless: we all know perfectly well that it is physiologically impossible for a ninety-year-old woman to give birth. We would then be left with a tale which is so inherently impossible that it cannot communicate any message about the faithfulness of God. It may have been easier for earlier generations to accept the historicity of this miracle, but the barrier is too high for us.

But it is precisely the impossibility of the story that makes the point – a point that remains valid today. God is faithful to his promise precisely in a situation that, according to human reasoning and all the evidence, makes it impossible for his word to be fulfilled. The narrative does not require us to believe in the historicity of certain events in the land of Canaan in the year 1800 BC.; the truth of its message has nothing to do with the question whether a particular ninety-year-old woman did in fact become a mother. The story in Genesis deliberately exaggerates the improbability – quite different in scale from the human improbability that women like Hannah (1 Sam 1) or Elizabeth (Lk 1), who are presumably around forty years old, can still become mothers – to the point of a sheer impossibility that underlines the sovereign transcendence of God's power to act in fulfilment of his promise. Where it is apparently crazy to hope, "Abraham *believed,* hoping against hope" (Rom 4:18) and saw the birth of Isaac.

The story of the birth of Isaac reveals to us that nothing is "too wonderful for the Lord" (Gen 18:14), and makes this point *in the context of his fidelity to his own word.* God does not work arbitrary miracles to display a meaningless power. He is active within history, and despite all obstacles, to manifest his faithfulness to the persons whom he loves, and to whom he has committed himself by calling them out of Haran in Chaldaea to the new land of Canaan. Because Abraham believed and hoped, even "against hope" as St Paul graphically puts it, he gave God space in which to act. We shall return to this theme in the next chapter, in which the apparent impossibility of God's fidelity to Abraham becomes even more dramatic. Let us conclude this chapter by reflecting on the significance of the new names given to Abram and Sarai.

* * *

For the Bible, a human name is often much more than merely a distinguishing label. It can contain a whole programme of life, as we see above all in the case of the Saviour: "You shall call his name Jesus" (i.e., "Yahweh saves"), "for it is he who shall save his people from their sins" (Mt 1:21). A change of name denotes a new spiritual beginning in a person's life: Simon is given the new name Cephas/Peter, since he is to be "the rock" on which Jesus builds his Church (Mt 16:18, Jn 1:42), Joseph the Levite joins the apostles in Jerusalem and receives the new name

Barnabas, interpreted as "son of consolation" (Acts 4:36). We see the same principle at work in a pagan context when Daniel is given a place at the court of King Nebuchadnezzar in Babylon and receives a new non-Hebrew name, Belteshazzar (Dan 1:7). In the case of the new names "Abraham" and "Sarah", God intervenes directly to replace the names once given by their human parents, underlining his initiative in their lives and their significance in salvation history.

In many religious families, the new member receives (or chooses) a new name at the beginning of the novitiate. This practice has become less frequent since the Council, and has been reversed in some communities, whose members have reverted to their baptismal names. The reason for this – apart from occasional difficulties with the civil authorities, who found it hard to know whether the same person was being talked about under two distinct names – is theological. It is a return to the traditional insight that the religious life is simply one way of living the baptismal Christian life, and that it is the baptismal name that is the truly *new* name. It is also possible to do both: my own religious family retains baptismal names, but some of my confrères add the name "Mary" when they take their vows (this sounds much less odd in French or German than in English).

One can argue in favour of either practice, because both are relativised by the eschatological new name which each of us will receive in heaven: "To the one who conquers I shall give a share in the hidden manna, and I shall give him a white stone, with a new name written on the stone which no one knows, except the one who receives it" (Rev 2:17). The number of names available on earth is limited; I am not the only person who bears my name, and so it is never capable of designating me and my vocation in an exclusive way. But this exclusiveness is promised us in heaven: there we shall not be interchangeable members of the chorus, but each one will receive "a new name which no one else knows".

* * *

A further element in a Christian name is very often significant: the element of patronage. This idea is often present at baptism, and is one reason why priests are reluctant to christen babies with names like "Elvis". It has also led in many countries to the practice of taking a saint's name at confirmation. A related example is that of Popes John Paul I and John Paul II, both of whom chose an explicitly programmatic name. When the Christian receives the name of a saint, a double relationship comes into being, intercession on the one hand and imitation on the other.

It is, of course, possible for me on earth to pray for "all mankind", for peace and righteousness in the whole world, for all the oppressed and all the persecuted. But the generic quality of this prayer does make it rather vague. The individual dimension in intercession is at least equally important; indeed, intercessory prayer for particular persons can be a specific vocation in the Church, as we see in St Monica (+ 387), whose vocation was to pray for the conversion of her husband and of her son Augustine. David Howard, an Anglican priest friend of mine who died in 1982, once wrote to me, "Let me know how you are getting on – with details. I need specific things to pray about!" The request surprised me at the time, but on reflection I saw how impeccably correct its theology was and how vague my own intercession usually was. I have no doubt at all that David keeps up his specific intercession for me in heaven – but not only for me.

For in heaven, the limitations on our knowledge of people that exist on earth cease to exist. I cannot know everyone here with the kind of intimacy that makes it possible to pray for "specific things". I cannot be acquainted to such a personal degree with what Vatican II called "the joy and hope, the grief and anguish of the people of our time" (*Gaudium et spes,* 1). But from heaven, freed from the boundaries of time and space, it is possible to know simultaneously the situations of an unlimited number of persons and to pray for each one of them in love. This is why one saint can be patron of very many persons, without this being reduced to a loose generic intercession for a group.

Father René Laurentin gives a suggestive image of this reality in his book about the phenomena of Medjugorje in the early years, before war broke out in Bosnia-Herzegovina. (I use the word "phenomena" deliberately, rather than "apparitions" or "revelations", in order to avoid expressing any kind of judgment about the authenticity of what is related. What interests me is the *image* he gives.) According to Laurentin, Our Lady speaks, not to the group as a group, but simultaneously to *each* of the group. She is, so to speak, carrying on five conversations at once. Whatever the Church eventually comes to say about the genuineness of Medjugorje, this is an extremely effective picture of what happens when a group of people pray at the same time: heaven does not take a "group" interest in them, but relates to each one individually.

From our side, the relationship with a patron involves imitation. This concept is easy enough to grasp when the patron is a well-known figure and one can read a biography. There is no problem with finding out about the life of St Ignatius of Loyola or St Teresa of Avila, for example; the problem is existential, the task of actually trying to put into practice what one has read. But what if my patron is a saint about whom little is known, or indeed nothing? Such saints are not lacking even in the general calendar of the Church – Blaise, for instance. It is hard to know what to say about him as a person when one blesses throats on his feast day! Or what of my own patron, Blessed Brian Lacey? It may be the case that a full biography of him is sitting in a library somewhere, but all I know about him is the date of his martyrdom, 10 December 1592. And if I know even that much, that is only because Brian was a popular boys' name in the 1950's, and thus three lines about him were included in a Catholic Truth Society pamphlet called "Saints' Names for Boys and Girls".

There is, however, another question: do I really need to know anything more about my patron than that?

"Imitation" does not mean the reproduction in the concrete historical circumstances of my life of what was present in the concrete historical circumstances of the life of my patron – any more than the "imitation" of Christ means the reproduction in our lives of the historical details of his life. It means something much simpler than that. It means that what was said of my patron can one day be said of me: here is a person who lived for God, consecrated to him in the community of the Church.

I recently visited a community of Brothers in Germany. In the course of evening prayer, they intercede for their dead confrères, some of whom died in the seventeenth century! Thus the names convey absolutely no associations or pictures to the members of the community today. The graves in their cemetery confine themselves to inscriptions bearing the name, date of birth, date of religious vows, and date of death. And it is this that can inspire me to imitate them. If I know that Brother Andrew and Sister Martha dedicated their lives to God and remained faithful to that dedication until their death, I know all I need to know. And I can hope that people will be able to say the same about me in fifty or a hundred and fifty years from now, when I am no more than a name in the necrology and a few dates in the cemetery. If indeed they can say that much about me, they will have said the essential thing, and they will be able to imitate me in the central fact of my life.

Graves in Italian cemeteries often have a photograph of the dead person to inform the living what he or she looked like. But the future of the overwhelming majority of us is to be completely forgotten. The memory of a very few people does last, "but of others there is no memory; they have perished as though they had never existed; they have become as though they had never been born, they and their children after them" (Sirach 44:9). These are not the makers of history, in human terms. But if, in their lives, God's salvation history became their personal history, then they are not forgotten, not absorbed into an impersonal mass of "humanity". God promises to each one of them "a new name which no one knows, except the one who receives it".

IV

The sacrifice of Abraham

Chapter 21 of Genesis seems to be the happy ending to the story of Abraham. Isaac is born, contrary to all human reasoning: God has shown the extraordinary power of his faithfulness to the one whom he had called and who had answered that call in faith. Potential loose ends in the story – their significance as threats shown by their presence in a variety of traditions in Genesis – are tied up when Ishmael is sent away and Abraham settles a quarrel about a well by making a covenant with the inhabitants of the land in which he is sojourning. At this point, when everything seems rosy, the peace is shattered:

"After these things God tested Abraham. He said to him, 'Abraham!' And he said, 'Here I am.' He said, 'Take your son, your only son Isaac, whom you love, and go to the land of Moriah, and offer him there as a burnt offering on one of the mountains that I shall show you'" (22:1f).

* * *

The first thing to be said about this commandment, which is so inconceivable to us (especially since we know the outcome of the story anyway, and therefore do not take the horrific words as seriously as we should), is that it is a perfectly *understandable* thing for God to require of Abraham. It fits in easily to the concepts of divinity and of human relationships to the divine which were current in Canaan. Human sacrifice was something *normal,* something that made perfect sense, within the existing religious framework. There are many references to human sacrifice in the Old Testament, most of them by means of the euphemism of "making someone pass through the fire", and it is specified that this practice belongs to the religions of Canaan. For example, we are told of the evil King Ahaz that "he did not do what was right in the sight of the Lord his God, as his ancestor David had done, but he walked in the way of the kings of Israel" (the northern kingdom which was regarded as semi-pagan by the south). "He even made his son pass through fire, according to the abominable practices of the nations whom the Lord drove out before the people of Israel. He sacrificed and made offerings on the high places, on the hills, and under every green tree" (2 Kings 16:2ff). Here we have the sacrifice of the king's supremely valuable possession, the heir to his throne, carried out in accordance with the religion of Canaan ("the nations whom the Lord drove out..."). The intense disapproval of the author of 2 Kings is clear. Yet it is also clear that he shares the belief of the Canaanite religion in the efficacy of human sacrifice, as we see in the story of the siege of the king of Moab (3:21ff). The Moabites are surrounded in Kirhareseth by the armies of Israel, Judah and Edom, and their situation is hopeless: "When the king of Moab saw that the battle was going against him, he took with him seven hundred swordsmen to break through, opposite the king of Edom; but they could not. *Then he took his firstborn son who was to succeed him, and offered him as a burnt offering on the wall.* And great wrath came upon Israel, so they withdrew from him and returned to their own land." It is perfectly clear that the author attributes Israel's retreat to this act of human sacrifice.

This is the background against which God's demand is to be understood, a background that we too easily forget because of its remoteness from the religious conceptions with which we operate. God's demand that Isaac, the only son, be offered as a burnt offering is understandable. He shows thereby that he is a god like the other gods who were venerated in Canaan, with the same rights.

But if it is understandable, this does not make it any the

less intolerable. For it is the annihilation, *by God himself,* of his own promises to Abraham. He had called Abram out of Haran and promised him descendants; he had refused to let Ishmael, the son born of human reasoning, be the heir promised, but had given Abram the new, programmatic name "father of a multitude", heightening the tension by promising that Sarah would bear a son in her extreme old age. And this apparently absurd promise is fulfilled: God displays his faithfulness.

Now, it is God himself who intervenes in Abraham's life to make a demand that tears up his promises and wipes out the proof of his faithfulness. For there is no promise that Sarah will bear Abraham another son to replace Isaac: God's demand is the simple destruction of what he himself has brought about. We can perhaps understand that a God who respects human freedom allows his salvific will to be thwarted – but what kind of God is this, who thwarts himself?

God does, of course, have a purpose in what he does here. But he does not as yet disclose this purpose to Abraham. He simply gives his intolerable commandment, overturning all that he has revealed of himself hitherto in his relationship with Abraham, as a challenge that Abraham must either accept or reject. If Abraham rejects God's commandment, he at least holds on to his only son Isaac; but if he accepts the commandment, all that his call has meant is now finished.

Abraham accepts, without saying a single word. On earlier occasions, he has protested that God's doings were inexplicable (cf. 15:2, quoted in the previous chapter). Now he only obeys, and without delay: "So Abraham rose early in the morning, saddled his donkey, and took two of his young men with him, and his son Isaac; he cut the wood for the burnt offering, and set out and went to the place in the distance that God had shown him" (22:3). We are told nothing of what Abraham "felt", no psychological analysis is offered. It would be easy to fill in the emotional details, if the author had wished to do so. But his only interest is to show us a man who obeys in faith, a man who does not question the apparently senseless command to sacrifice his own son. At the one point where emotions could easily have intruded into the narrative, they are pruned back with an extraordinary sobriety: "Isaac said to his father Abraham, 'Father!' And he said, 'Here I am, my son.' He said, 'The fire and the wood are here, but where is the lamb for a burnt offering?' Abraham said, 'God himself will provide the lamb for a burnt offering, my son.' So the two of them walked on together." Abraham obeys.

* * *

The outcome of the story is the unexpected reaffirmation of God's faithfulness: God does indeed provide the victim for the sacrifice, but it is not Isaac. An angel calls out to Abraham, "Do not lay your hand on the boy or do anything to him", and Abraham sees a ram, which he offers "as a burnt offering instead of his son". God is not arbitrary like a Canaanite god who demands the sacrifice of a king's heir: he acts in love and fidelity, even if this will be perceived only *after* the demand has been made and has been accepted by the one he calls. God's action here is a "testing" of Abraham (cf. 22:1), and at the crucial moment the angel says, "Now I know that you fear God, since you have not withheld your son, your only son, from me." Why is this testing necessary?

It is not necessary in order for God to be "sure" of Abraham's trust in him; God can read our hearts, and he does not need to carry out experiments on us. The testing serves another purpose: it is designed to deepen the original "yes" which Abram said in response to God's call and invitation.

It does not cost very much to *say* "yes" to God, just as it does not cost very much to *write* a cheque. The decisive question about the cheque is whether I have the funds in my bank account to cover it, and the decisive question about my "yes" to God is whether it is covered by an affirmation at a sufficiently deep level in me to make it a *genuine* acceptance of his call. But this deep level in me is not something that is attained all at once: even if my "yes" is perfectly sincere, spoken in faith and trust and love, it still takes time to permeate the whole of my being. In precisely the same way, the "yes" which husband and wife say to each other in their wedding ceremony may be the perfectly sincere expression of their mutual commitment in love, but it takes time to permeate the whole of their being as individuals and make them a *couple,* a family, on the truly deep level. The same can be said of the "yes" that is said to God at religious profession or ordination.

God is endlessly patient with us, and he does not demand that we shall run before we can walk. The principle of all vocations is that they grow: and this means, at least ideally, that we never stop growing. There is always a deeper level on which I can repeat my initial "yes" to God – though this repetition is not a reproduction, as if one had to try to recapture emotional states of one's younger self. Within the continuity of my life, organically linked to what has gone before, there is an authentically new "yes" to be spoken today. This principle of growth means that, even when one has to give up one sphere of activity, one need not stagnate. A friend once told me that her grandmother had discovered a new "usefulness" at the age of ninety-three: "Young people from the church come to visit her, and she prays with them." I myself have seen how a woman of ninety-eight, to whom I used to bring communion, was still growing in faith. Such people are no doubt exceptional, but the principle they embody ought to be entirely normal in the Christian life: one never stops growing. St Augustine affirms that stagnation is impossible here – one is always *en route,* either towards God or away from him.

This growth is not a linear progress. The physical and especially the emotional development of a human person

41

are not a linear progress that makes unwaveringly for its goal. We grow through mastering crises, and these crises can knock us badly off-course for long periods of time. Abraham's "yes" to his vocation is tested in the two crises we have seen in these chapters, Sarah's childlessness and the command to offer his son as a burnt offering. In each case, his renewed "yes" expressed in his faith in the God who has spoken to him and called him is rewarded by the renewed divine affirmation of his vocation: here God says, "By myself I have sworn, says the Lord: Because you have done this, and have not withheld your son, your only son, I will indeed bless you, and I will make your off-spring as numerous as the stars of heaven and as the sand that is on the seashore... *because you have obeyed my voice*" (22:16ff).

As I have said, the author of Genesis portrays Abraham as the one who obeys. He does not show us a man who is knocked off-course, even momentarily, by the demands God makes of him. We shall see in chapter VI, in the case of Jeremiah, how the basic message of Genesis is deepened when the psychological problems involved in this quality of obedience make themselves felt. For the present, how-ever, the outlines of this fundamentally important message are clear. Let us take up one final point.

* * *

We have seen that God's demand that Isaac be sacri-ficed was a demand that made sense in its religious context. This was the kind of thing a god had the right to require of one who believed in him.

God did not in fact desire the sacrifice of the son of the promise. But what if he had? Would we be justified in saying that his demand was excessive?

In the case of a human sacrifice, we certainly should be justified in reacting like this. But if we transfer the history of Abraham and Isaac into our own lives, how are we to react when God asks of us something that is incomprehensible or even apparently crazy? What if my superiors tell me that they wish to move me from one place or one kind of work to another? What if I find myself in a situation in which my particular gifts have no opportunity whatever of contributing to the kingdom of God? Such questions are not theoretical: there must be very few religious congregations indeed that have never misused, under-used, or utterly frustrated the gifted persons who have entered them – appealing then to the virtues of humility and obedience to cover up their mistakes.

The figure of Jeremiah will help us to see more fully the dimensions of this problem – not only the human suffering, but also the questions it poses to our understanding of God as a God of love and faithfulness. The figure of Abraham tells us something fundamental, even if it leaves open the questions that have just been asked: it tells us that if God is genuinely "the Lord" of my life, then he has in principle the right to demand *everything* from me, including life itself (in martyrdom). If I have said "yes" in the sacrament of confirmation to my baptismal covenant, and if I have then further specified this in the "yes" of marriage or ordination or religious vows, then he has the right to "cash the cheque" which I have made out to him. It is not hard to let God be "the Lord" when he asks only easy things, things one would quite like to have done anyway – if you like children, you are not going to find it difficult to obey Mother Superior when she assigns you to work in the kindergarten. But God does have the right to ask everything of me.

I experienced this principle once when I was asked to take over a parish in the depths of the countryside and arrived to find the house totally empty of furniture. The previous priest had taken everything with him except for a chair and the telephone (which was sitting on the floor). My initial reaction was to be furious. Then I went into the church to prepare for Mass, and suddenly reflected, "But after all, you have taken a vow of poverty. Doesn't God have the right to let you experience genuine poverty for once, instead of the comfort of a monastery?" It was a revelation of how little I was prepared to let God truly be "the Lord" of the life that I had consecrated to him. After I had been given that insight, I became calm and celebrated the Mass with the people who had come to church. Then I discovered that the Bishop had arranged for furniture to be sent, and that I would after all have a bed to sleep in.

If God does exercise his right to demand everything from us, he does not act arbitrarily. As we see in the case of Abraham, he acts in fidelity and love. We can therefore believe that even the heaviest sacrifices do have a meaning, and that this meaning is positive.

But we may see this meaning only much later on; indeed, we may see it only after this life. For example, many Christians from the very earliest days have been called to die for their faith in Jesus. He himself predicts persecution (e.g., Mk 13:9), and this is a prominent theme of the Book of Revelation. The New Testament promises victory to those who accept this suffering; and it is easy enough for us today to look back over the broad sweep of history and say that "the blood of the martyrs is the seed of the Church". But those who are actually suffering persecution and martyrdom may well have the greatest difficulty in seeing anything positive for the Church in their experience. This is why they may be tempted to compromise with the persecutors in the hope of preserving at least something, rather than see the obliteration of the Church's life (and this is why some of the Orthodox bishops in Russia and Catholic "peace priests" in Hungary and Czechoslovakia collaborated with communist regimes). There is an even greater difficulty when they know that their martyrdom will be twisted and misrepresented by the propaganda of their persecutors, in such a way that no one will believe it truly *was* a martyrdom (as happens at the end of Graham Greene's *The Honorary Consul*). Archbishop Oscar Romero (+ 1980) is now pretty universally honoured as a martyr, and the cause of his beatification has been introduced. But his death, like that of many of the martyrs of the Reformation period, was misrepresented as a purely political event; and his posthumously published diaries show how much he was wilfully misunderstood and vilified within the Church during his lifetime: he saw his social involvement as a testimony to Jesus Christ, but they dismissed it as a leftwing political activism that betrayed the Gospel. In such circumstances, to say "yes" to God means the darkness of naked faith. For it is all too easy to see one's suffering and death as the triumph of evil over good.

For those who are persecuted, as for us in the much less dramatic lives we have consecrated to Christ, Abraham is to be followed as the man who believed and "hoped against hope". He experienced God's faithfulness to his word. If we too are faithful, despite the cost, then we too will see the same faithfulness. The guarantee of this is, of course, not to be found in the story of Abraham himself, but in the story of Jesus: because the Father "did not spare his own Son, but gave him up for us all" (Rom 8:32), thereby utterly outdoing Abraham and any of us in the measure of his sacrifice and gift, *nothing* "will be able to separate us from the love of God which is in Christ Jesus our Lord" (8:39). We shall return to this theme after we have reflected on the call of Moses.

V

The call of Moses

Abraham is mentioned twice each day in the public liturgy of the Church, in the New Testament canticles of the Divine Office. In each case, to speak of Abraham is to speak of God's fidelity. The Magnificat at evening prayer speaks of "the mercy promised to our fathers, to Abraham and his sons for ever", and the Benedictus at morning prayer recalls: "He swore to Abraham our father to grant us, that free from fear, and saved from the hands of our foes, we might serve him in holiness and justice." We have seen in the last three chapters God's fidelity to Abraham during his lifetime. The Benedictus recalls the fidelity to Abraham beyond his death. The structure of the story is basically the same: in a situation of apparent impossibility, God takes the initiative to show that he keeps his word.

When Abram came into Canaan, God promised, "To your offspring I will give this land" (Gen 12:7). This promise is repeated to Abraham several times, and is confirmed to Isaac (cf. 26:4) and to Jacob, Isaac's heir: "I am the Lord, the God of Abraham your father and the God of Isaac; the land on which you lie I will give to you and to your offspring" (28:13). However, when the Book of Exodus opens, several hundred years have passed, and the descendants of Abraham are slaves in Egypt. There seems no human possibility of their possessing the promised land.

Now God intervenes by calling Moses. He appears to him in the burning bush at Horeb and offers him a wholly new relationship to his God by revealing the divine name, "I am who am" (Ex 3:14). This is not a private spiritual experience for Moses: he is sent on a mission. "I have observed the misery of my people who are in Egypt; I have

47

heard their cry on account of their taskmasters. Indeed, I know their sufferings, and I have come down to deliver them... So come, *I will send you to Pharaoh to bring my people, the Israelites, out of Egypt*" (3:7ff). Moses' ministry in delivering Israel will be God's own work of deliverance. God four times calls himself "the God of your father(s), the God of Abraham, the God of Isaac, and the God of Jacob", emphasising his faithfulness to those to whom he had revealed himself in the past; and when this passage is read in the broader context of the Pentateuch as a whole, it can be seen as the fulfilment of God's promise to Abraham that "Your offspring shall be aliens in a land that is not theirs, and shall be slaves there, and they shall be oppressed for four hundred years; but I will bring judgment on the nation that they serve, and afterward they shall come out" (Gen 15:13f).

The same point is made later in the Pentateuch, in Moses' speech to the people before they enter the land of promise: "It was not because you were more numerous than any other people that the Lord set his heart on you and chose you – for you were the fewest of all peoples. It was because the Lord loved you and *kept the oath that he swore to your ancestors,* that the Lord has brought you out with a mighty hand, and redeemed you from the house of slavery, from the hand of Pharaoh king of Egypt" (Deut 7:7f).

* * *

Apart from the message of God's tenacious fidelity to his word, the story of the call of Moses has other significant lessons to teach us about our own call.

First, Moses reacts with shock to God's charge to him, because he sees himself as unqualified: "O my Lord, I have never been eloquent, neither in the past nor even now that you have spoken to your servant; but I am slow of speech and slow of tongue" (Ex 4:10). God's reply is sharply dismissive of this objection: "Who gives speech to mortals?

Who makes them mute or deaf, seeing or blind? Is it not I, the Lord? Now go, and I will be with your mouth and teach you what you are to speak." Moses' reaction is the reaction of one who thinks that he himself will bear responsibility for what he must do and say, and who realises his incapacity. But he must learn that the work he does is God's, and that therefore God will bear the responsibility for its success.

The same point is made in the story (handed on in various versions) about Pope John XXIII, who was unable to get to sleep one night early in his pontificate because of his worries about the Church. But finally the Holy Spirit intervened and said, "Who is in charge of the Church, you or me?" And when the Pope acknowledged, "You, of course", he fell asleep at once.

We were not called because of our exceptional capabilities, as if we were candidates before a selection panel. God has taken the free initiative in calling us, for reasons that he alone knows – the old Missal said that popes were "chosen according to thy mysterious design", and we can all apply these unflattering words to ourselves! But this means that he commits himself to us. We can trust that he will be at work *in* our work, just as he delivered Israel by means of the ministry of the tongue-tied Moses. St Paul calls himself a "fellow-worker with God" (cf. 1 Cor 3:9), but there is surely a deeper sense in which we can say that God is our "fellow-worker". Our incapacity is no barrier to his purposes: "I will be with your mouth and teach you what you are to speak."

The crucial question for us is whether we have the humility to say, with Mary in the Magnificat, "He who is mighty has done great things for me", or whether it is our wish to be able to say, "I have done great things for him". If the second alternative is our basic understanding of our ministry in the Church, we shall never bear the fruit that we could have borne if we had made of our lives a space for *God* to work.

* * *

Second, as I have written, the encounter with God in the burning bush is simultaneously a mission. Moses' meeting with the Lord is a service of God's people, not his own private spiritual concern. His whole life is set at their service – not just his "work" of delivering them.

This applies to everyone whom God calls. A vocation is a gift to the Church, not primarily a gift to the individual who is called; and since the Church in turn exists for the world, not for itself, a vocation is a gift to the whole world, whether or not those we serve believe in God. The logic of the fulfilment offered by such a life is not the logic of a society which (as I once heard it put in a sermon) understands "fulfilment" in terms of "fill-full-ment". We are indeed "filled full", but not by heaping up spiritual possessions for ourselves (as we "collected indulgences" when I was a child). We are filled by emptying ourselves out totally in service of others. This implies the commitment of the whole of our being.

It is important to emphasise this, because there is an ingrained misunderstanding which leads us to evaluate people according to factors that are visible and quantifiable. It may be their prayer, as when one hears that some community "prays for eight hours a day!" More commonly, it is their work. Religious women have often been regarded primarily as cheap labour, valued both inside and outside their own congregation for their work capacity and consequently made to feel useless when illness or old age made them unable to contribute to the congregation's work. "Yes, isn't it wonderful – Sister is eighty, and she still takes her turn at night duty in the wards!" This praise contains a nasty implication, which I once heard put into words by a Mother Provincial who, on hearing that one of my confrères was seriously ill and not expected to be able to resume his duties, observed coldly, "Sick people are out of place in a monastery." She could doubtless have made her own what

St Pius X (+ 1914) said: "We are not ordained priests to have a comfortable life, but to work hard and die of exhaustion!"

Obviously, work is an exceedingly important dimension of a person's identity (I shall return to this point in chapter X below). And Paul insists that those who are unwilling to work "should not eat" (2 Thess 3:10). But when the Book of Revelation says that "the works of those who die in the Lord follow along with them" into heaven (14:13), this means much more than just the individual things done in the name of Jesus. It refers to the totality of the life that has been lived here on earth. This is why we must not isolate one quantifiable and visible activity.

This whole way of looking at things is highly dangerous, for it is essentially worldly. A person is valued for measurable external abilities, whereas the true "contribution to the kingdom of God" consists in a gift of self that is not tied to any specific activities in prayer or work, and can be required of a sick or elderly person just as much as of one who is young and healthy. It is an *expropriation of myself,* so that the centre of gravity in my life is *displaced from myself* to the God who calls me to himself and simultaneously sends me out to my brothers and sisters. The whole of my life – prayer and work and rest and illness – is meant to be a self-emptying that brings me fulfilment.

There lies a fundamental temptation here for Christians. We live in a society which tolerates us – no one is going to be put in prison in north-west Europe or northern America for professing faith in Jesus Christ. But at the same time, our society *marginalises* us in a kind of "Native American reservation", since (as I have said above) the highly complex modern cultures in which we live are governed by ways of thinking and economic and political processes for which faith in God and a living relationship to Jesus Christ are – not denied, but "irrelevant". Our lives are thus compartmentalised: religion is just one "sector" of what we do, and it does not impinge greatly on the other "sectors".

This makes it immensely difficult to retain the biblical outlook which sees God addressing the wholeness of the person and expecting a response from this totality. The task is all the more difficult because what Paul calls "conformation to this world" in which we live (Rom 12:2) is an imperceptible process today.

This second reflection on the biblical narrative of Moses' call may prompt the question: How much is my life an *integrated gift of my whole self* to God and to my neighbour?

* * *

Third, the call of Moses shows us the link between vocation and worship. When God calls him from the burning bush, he says, "Come no closer! Remove the sandals from your feet, for the place on which you are standing is holy ground" (Ex 3:5). The external gesture denotes an internal preparation to encounter the holiness of God; this gesture has been preserved above all in Islam, but it is not unknown among Christians – I have seen Indian priests celebrating Mass barefoot in Rome. We do something basically similar when we bless ourselves with holy water on entering a church. A vocation is always an encounter with the holiness of God, calling forth in us a specifically *religious* response. In other words, it is not like the choice of a profession, but is the deeply personal response of committing one's life in love to the Lord,

Just as Moses' life is to be poured out in serving the people of God, so too his encounter in worship on Mount Horeb is to include the people: "I will be with you," says God, "and this shall be the sign for you that it is I who sent you: when you [singular] have brought the people out of Egypt, *you [plural] shall worship God on this mountain*" (3:12). When Moses and Aaron go to Pharaoh, they tell him that they want to lead out the Israelites for a great act of worship: "Let us go a three days' journey into the wilderness to sacrifice to the Lord our God" (5:3). This will be the true liberation for the people.

When the Second Vatican Council calls the liturgy the "peak" or "high point" – *culmen,* from which the English word "culmination" comes – of the Church's life, this implies that the Church exists to worship God and that evangelisation finds its goal in the sharing by all people in the prayer, and especially in the eucharist, of Christ's mystical body. Whether or not a particular vocation is directed to the evangelisation of others, we must all evangelise ourselves in this matter: in other words, we must remind ourselves how important it is for us to pray.

This is not by any means as obvious in our daily living as it is on the level of principle. My impression both from my own life and from many conversations with other Christians (including contemplative nuns) is that prayer *always* gets pushed aside in favour of other activities. Our time is the most precious thing we have, and we allocate it consistently to other things than the direct encounter with God in prayer.

To a large extent, this is because we are afraid of exposing ourselves to God in prayer – and of exposing ourselves to ourselves. It is a very common experience that no sooner do we begin to pray, than all kinds of distractions pop up. These may be quite trivial thoughts about what we are going to eat for supper, or they may be important problems that we ought to take directly into our prayer. But sometimes much more unpleasant things surface from our depths. Usually, as the desert fathers tell us, these take the forms of vivid sexual images or intense surges of aggression against specific persons. These are in fact a thoroughly positive sign that our relationship with God is moving into our depths and stirring up the mud! But since this process is so deep and so disturbing, we prefer not to take the risk of exposing ourselves to it. And so we take refuge in good and useful activities; if we know the tradition, we manipulate it to justify ourselves.

For example, St Philip Neri (+ 1595) said that "If we leave off prayer when we are called to perform some work of love for our neighbour, we do not really leave prayer: we leave Christ for the sake of Christ."

Then there is the story of St Silvanus in the fourth century. One day two Messalian monks come to visit him, and are scandalised to see his monks engaged in manual work. They reprimand him by means of two quotations from the Gospels: "Do not work for the food that perishes! Mary has chosen the better part" (Jn 6:27; Lk 10:42). Silvanus assigns the visitors a cell and gives them a book to read. They are then left in peace all day – no one comes to fetch them for the one meal that is taken at three in the afternoon. Finally they themselves go in search of the abbot to ask if the monks have not eaten that day. "Certainly," replies Silvanus. "But why did you not call us?" And Silvanus looks at them calmly and says, "You are spiritual men and do not need this food... you have chosen the better part." This story became the classic illustration of the dangers of over-spiritualising the spiritual life, of over-emphasising the role of prayer (which the Messalians were accused of doing).

But while what Philip Neri and Silvanus say is entirely correct, we must not forget that the speakers are both men who spent very large portions of their day in prayer. They are a world away from the justification of activism, of neglecting prayer altogether in favour of "useful" work. They knew that if activity is to bear fruit for the kingdom, it must come from a life anchored in the encounter with the Lord who has called us to serve him. It is too easy, if one is a religious, to tell oneself that prayer in common with one's community is enough; it is too easy, if one is a priest, to operate a curious switching-off mechanism whereby one celebrates Masses and other rites "for" other people, without actually praying *with* those present.

Quantity can, of course, have a deadening effect. It is hard to imagine how mediaeval monks coped psychologically with the tremendous quantity of vocal prayer their Rule imposed on them. In my own experience, I can say that I did not find it easy to be fully present in all the worship of a typical Sunday in my Italian parish, with three Masses, two hours in the confessional, five baptisms and occasionally a long procession with a statue of Our Lady thrown in for good measure. On top of that, there was the Divine Office, which I prayed with a confrère. I began to see the point of St Pius X's dictum about dying of exhaustion. But I also began to see that the rhythm of my prayer life is not necessarily the rhythm of one day at a time. That kind of Sunday simply does not permit one to go in for long private prayer or spiritual reading. But after Sunday comes Monday: if we take a week as our unit, it becomes much easier to organise our time in such a way that prayer finds a genuinely central place within the whole arc of seven days. This may require organisation. Gisbert Greshake makes the practical suggestion in his book *Priestersein* that we should fill in slots for prayer in our appointments diary, and that we should keep them, just as we keep the slots we have filled in for meetings and other "activities".

We must, in short, evangelise ourselves and bring ourselves to the encounter with God which is the beginning of our vocation and must be its continuous driving force. Exodus says that "the Lord used to speak to Moses face to face, as one speaks to a friend" (33:11). This is an essential element of every ministry in the Church. If we do not give God the chance to do this, we shall never know the one whom we seek to serve.

* * *

In chapter III, I spoke briefly about intercession. The figure of Moses helps us to see more clearly the link between intercessory prayer and every Christian vocation (not just specific calls like St Monica's).

Moses' relationship with God in prayer takes on a new dimension while he is on Mount Sinai and the people begin to worship a golden calf. The Lord says to him, "Your people, whom you brought up out of the land of Egypt, have acted perversely... I have seen this people, how stiff-necked they are. Now let me alone, so that my wrath may burn hot against them and I may consume them; and of you I will make a great nation" (Ex 32:7ff). God's anger and his decision, with its offer to Moses, may seem understandable. But Moses protests, reminding God of his own word, spoken in the past: "Turn from your fierce wrath; change your mind and do not bring disaster on your people. Remember Abraham, Isaac, and Israel, your servants, how you swore to them by your own self, saying to them, 'I will multiply your descendants like the stars of heaven, and all this land that I have promised I will give to your descendants, and they shall inherit it for ever'" (32:12f). God accepts Moses' prayer: "And the Lord changed his mind about the disaster that he planned to bring on his people" (32:14).

What is happening in this story?

First, it is clear that God does not "change his mind" in the literal sense, as if he were to "repent" and abandon his plans on hearing Moses' arguments. Such an understanding of God reduces him to the level of a human dialogue-partner. This may not be clear to Moses himself, who goes so far as to appeal to God's *amour propre*: if he destroys the people whom he himself has freed from slavery, the Egyptians will mock him (32:12). Such an argument might carry weight with a human king who was threatening to carry out a massacre, but the true argument on which Moses relies is implicit in his reference to Abraham, Isaac and Jacob: were God to destroy his people, then he would show himself to be unfaithful to his own promise. He would in fact be contradicting his own nature and destroying his own work of liberation.

But second, and more significantly for us, God has no

intention of destroying the sinful people. It is he who tells Moses about them and (the word is not too strong) *provokes him* to intercede for them that they may be spared. This has a double effect: it affects the people, in that they are in fact spared when Moses "stands in the breach before God for them" (cf. Ps 106:23) by taking the risk of protesting and correcting God himself. And it affects Moses, in that he is drawn more deeply into the spiritual dimension of his ministry. It is not only through political and military acts that Moses is to free Israel: through his intercession, he frees them from being punished for falling away from God. Moses' intercession is an integral part of the work that God wills to carry out through his ministry. It is he who inspires this new dimension in Moses' vocation.

For us too, intercessory prayer is an integral part of the vocation to which God has called us. Whatever forms our particular ministry may take, we are all called to offer the Lord our intercession as a means whereby he can build up his kingdom. Intercession remains profoundly mysterious. We cannot explain satisfactorily how it helps another person. But the example of Moses – and above all, naturally, the example of Jesus who prayed for his disciples – shows us the salvific character of intercessory prayer. And occasionally God does lift the veil and show us with unmistakable clarity that such intercession is inspired by him, and that we should always follow the instinct to pray for someone. Since I do not wish to close this chapter with a vague general assertion, let me conclude with two examples from my own experience which have confirmed the point for me.

A good many years ago, I was taking part in a theological conference in Vienna as secretary. One afternoon, while writing up the minutes in my room, I suddenly felt the urge to pray for my uncle – without at all seeing any reason why I should do so. I did pray for him, and then went on with my work. A few days later, I arrived home in Scotland and my mother greeted me with the words, "You must pray for your uncle – he has had a stroke." I then discovered that he had had his stroke precisely at the time when I, very far away, had felt moved to pray for him.

The second example happened on 9 March 1988 in Oslo. I felt strongly inclined to preach at Mass about the Forty Martyrs of Sebaste, who are commemorated on that date in the Byzantine Rite. Reflection said to me that I should preach about the Gospel of the day instead, partly because it is good to do so anyway in Lent, but even more basically because I thought the idea too exotic. What on earth did Armenian martyrs of the early fourth century have to do with the contemplative nuns of Norway to whom I would be preaching? Better to keep my feet on the ground. It was literally only as I made my way to the lectern that I made up my mind to follow my inclination, and I preached about the martyrs, inviting the nuns to pray for the Churches in Armenia. Half an hour after the end of Mass, I watched the television news, and the first item concerned the rioting in Azerbaijan in which Christian Armenians had been massacred...

In each case, God inspired in me a prayer of intercession which he then took up into his own purposes. What my prayer may have "achieved" is his mystery; I can quite safely be agnostic about such questions. But these experiences, which can be paralleled in so many people's lives, have underlined for me the importance of always following the inclinations one feels to make intercession, because the source of these inclinations is the Lord. Such prayer belongs in a profound way to the Christian calling.

* * *

It can happen that God tells me that one particular intercessory prayer is not a part of my vocation. Here, it is not the prayer that is problematic in itself – it is always good to pray for the persons and situations that concern us. But we pray: "May *your* will be done". The substance of intercession is not to be merely the proclamation of *my* will vis-à-vis God.

I remember once sitting by the bedside of a friend who was dying a slow and painful death. I held his hand and prayed, over and over again for about two hours: "Let him die! Let him die!" This was the expression of my friendship, of my love of neighbour: it is natural to want to spare others suffering, and to express this in our prayer. But when I came out of the hospital and waited for the bus that would take me home, I heard God say to me very clearly: "And what business is it of *yours*, when he dies?"

This was (to put it mildly) a shock. "God is love," says John, and we tend to take our own love as the model when we attempt to understand the divine love. But sometimes he lets us experience how radically different his love is from ours. But if it demands more than our human love, this is possible only because God is able to give those he loves infinitely more than we can give them. If we believe this, we can also accept that in some situations "we do not know how to pray as we ought" (Rom 8:26). Our love must be content to say: "Even if I do not understand it, may your will be done anyway" – just as Jesus prayed in Gethsemane.

VI
Jeremiah's call

"Before I formed you in the womb I knew you, and before you were born I consecrated you; I appointed you a prophet to the nations" (Jer 1:5).

Jeremiah's vocation is something that lies in God's eternal plan. From all eternity, God knows what he will do for his people, and this foreknowledge involves the calling of a particular person, "Jeremiah, son of Hilkiah, of the priests who were in Anathoth in the land of Benjamin... in the days of King Josiah son of Amon of Judah" (1:1f). It is not as if a sudden emergency had come up, and God had to cast about for someone to save the situation: no, "*before* you were born I consecrated you". Jeremiah is not interchangeable. It is precisely as Jeremiah, here and now, that he serves God's eternal plan. The same is true of everyone whom God calls: we are not interchangeable pawns on his chessboard, but each of us has a distinct and irreplaceable ministry which no one else can carry out in the same time and place. This is the measureless dignity of every vocation, however modest it may seem.

I once asked a prayer group in my Italian parish, "Who is more important in the Church, the Pope or our sacristan – *il papa* or *Peppina?*" As devout Catholics, they answered with a single voice, "*Il papa!*" I replied, "Well, if the Pope dies tomorrow, we shall have a new one next week. But if Peppina dies, who will take care of the sacristy here?" I trust that they got the message: we cannot use criteria of external visibility to evaluate the relative importance of the ministries that God gives his Church. Each one has its own specific importance, which is not replaceable by any other: for just as our sacristan Peppina was not called to carry out the ministry of Pope, so John Paul II was not called to carry out the ministry of sacristan in our parish. Neither is more "important" than the other.

Indeed, those whose charism most builds up the Church may be completely unknown to the Church itself. Hans Urs von Balthasar (+ 1988) once suggested that the greatest saint of all those portrayed in the New Testament might well be the widow who put her two copper coins into the temple treasury (Mk 12:41ff): only God knows her name.

Each one of us is called to serve God in a wholly specific ministry, for which we were chosen "before I formed you in the womb... before you were born". The divine initiative expressed in these words is underlined when Jeremiah protests: "Ah, Lord God! Truly I do not know how to speak, for I am only a boy." God's reply here is even sharper than his rebuke to Moses on Mount Horeb, which we read in the last chapter: "Do not say, 'I am only a boy'; for you shall go to all to whom I send you, and you shall speak whatever I command you. Do not be afraid of them, for I am with you to deliver you, says the Lord" (Jer 1:7f). The prophet's "I" must give place to God's "I": "I send you... I command you... I am with you". The following gesture makes this even clearer: "Then the Lord put out his hand and touched my mouth; and the Lord said to me, 'Now I have put my words in your mouth. See, today I appoint you over nations and over kingdoms...'" To be set over nations and kingdoms is, of course, to take the place that belongs to God, but not to "usurp" this place: the ministry of Jeremiah is to be the *vehicle through which God acts in history*. And God is a God who is faithful: "I am watching over my word to perform it" (1:12).

God reaffirms his protection of Jeremiah, who is entrusted with a highly dangerous task: "I for my part have made you today a fortified city, an iron pillar, and a bronze wall, against the whole land – against the kings of Judah, its princes, its priests, and the people of the land. They will fight against you; but they shall not prevail against you, for *I am with you,* says the Lord, to deliver you" (1:18f).

The narrative sections of the Book of Jeremiah show us how violent and dangerous was the opposition provoked by his prophesying. But always he is protected. For example, when Uriah the son of Shemaiah prophesies "in words exactly like those of Jeremiah" and is put to death by King Jehoiakim, "the hand of Ahikam son of Shaphan was with Jeremiah so that he was not given over into the hands of the people to be put to death" (26:20ff). He is helped later by the court officials (cf. 36:19), by Ebedmelech the eunuch (38:7ff), and even by King Zedekiah (37:16ff). When the Lord has demonstrated the truth of his word which Jeremiah had preached, by handing over the unrepentant city to the armies of the Chaldaeans, he also demonstrates the truth of his promise to Jeremiah himself. He is neither killed nor deported to Babylon, but is allowed by the victors to remain in the land (39:11ff). As God had told him, "They will fight against you; but they shall not prevail against you, for I am with you, says the Lord, to deliver you." Humanly speaking, the odds against Jeremiah are overwhelming: he compares himself to "a gentle lamb led to the slaughter" (11:19). But God is faithful and rescues him from all the plots against him.

* * *

Were this the whole message of the Book of Jeremiah, it would take us no further than the message given us in the story of Abram: namely, that God, who takes the initiative in calling a person to carry out the divine work in history, shows his fidelity in protecting his minister. There is, however, a new dimension in Jeremiah which takes our reflections on to a significantly deeper level. In Jeremiah's prayer at 20:7ff we see the psychological cost that is involved for him in remaining faithful to his calling.

Jeremiah has been ordered by the Lord to go to Topheth and utter a prophecy of doom. He returns to the city and likewise prophesies doom in the court of the temple. The chief officer of the temple, the priest Pashhur, beats him and puts him in the stocks. This experience of the apparent futility of his prophesying provokes a crisis in the prophet: "O Lord, you have enticed me, and I was enticed; you have overpowered me, and you have prevailed." For now Jeremiah can see – at least, so he believes – that God's word was not true. God had promised to protect him against all who would resist his message, but now: "I have become a laughingstock all day long; everyone mocks me... For I hear many whispering... All my close friends are watching for me to stumble. 'Perhaps he can be enticed, and we can prevail against him, and take our revenge on him'." Indeed, "the word of the Lord has become for me a reproach and derision all day long."

This is the situation, as Jeremiah sees it. God has called him and then has failed him.

His prayer shows three emotional reactions to this situation: the first is the obvious idea that, since no one listens to him and all pour scorn on his prophecy, he should simply stop: "I will not mention him, or speak any more in his name." But here the prophet finds that the awareness of his vocation is too strong for him: "Then within me there is something like a burning fire shut up in my bones; I am weary with holding it in, and I cannot." Jeremiah *must* speak. He cannot hold this fire within him, for it is too powerful. The calculation of human reason, urging silence in the face of hostility and of actual physical danger, is overwhelmed by the elemental force of his vocation. God says to him in another passage, "Is not my word like fire, and like a hammer that breaks a rock in pieces?" (23:29); here, the rock broken to pieces is the prophet Jeremiah himself. Despite what his reason tells him, he must speak out.

The second reaction we find in the prayer at 20:7ff is to

recall the promise and the power of the Lord: "But the Lord is with me like a dread warrior; therefore my persecutors will stumble, and they will not prevail." And so Jeremiah can break into a song of thanksgiving: "Sing to the Lord; praise the Lord! For he has delivered the life of the needy from the hands of evildoers."

Were this the end of the prayer, we might find it edifying: the prophet has overcome his doubts and, in the midst of his sufferings, has found words of praise and confidence in his Lord: "for to you I have committed my cause". But abruptly, without any transition, the prayer changes key, so that we have the third reaction – bitterness and depression. Here there is nothing that we are likely to find "edifying": "Cursed be the day on which I was born! The day when my mother bore me, let it not be blessed! Cursed be the man who brought the news to my father, saying, 'A child is born to you, a son,' making him very glad. Let that man be like the cities that the Lord overthrew without pity" (i.e., Sodom and Gomorrah, as related in Gen 19), "because he did not kill me in the womb; so my mother would have been my grave, and her womb forever great. Why did I come forth from the womb to see toil and sorrow, and spend my days in shame?"

What is going on in this text? How are the second and third reactions to Jeremiah's situation related to each other? Does his thanksgiving for deliverance simply flicker out, so that despair has the last word? But what then of the fire that is within him, forcing him to prophesy? Is his prophesying merely an act of self-destruction? Or has the textual tradition of this chapter perhaps mixed up the paragraphs of the prayer, so that the true order of reactions ought after all to be "edifying": first the realisation that he cannot keep silence, then a momentary despair, and finally confident praise and thanksgiving for deliverance? What, ultimately, is the logic of this prayer? What is happening in it?

The answer is that there is no logical progression in Jeremiah's prayer. The second and third reactions – deep emotions of thanksgiving, confidence, bitterness, despair – are set side by side in the text because they coexist in Jeremiah. One may give way to the other, but then it returns again in strength. And the reasoning mind, which would short-circuit this emotional drain by refusing to speak any more in the name of the Lord, is over-ruled from outside itself, by the "burning fire shut up in my bones". Anyone who has experienced this kind of rapid alternation of deep emotions knows the pain Jeremiah is going through, and can therefore also appreciate both the negative cry of the opening – "You have enticed (or, seduced) me!" – and the positive cry of triumph in verse 13 – "Sing to the Lord, praise the Lord!" There is no logic that can hold these together – the only "logical" thing would be to abandon the vocation which has led Jeremiah into this conflict of emotional reactions!

What can we learn from this for our own response to God's calling?

* * *

The first and most obvious point is the lesson that *we must hang on*. And we must do this, not out of human obstinacy, but because in us too there is a "fire" which is so strong that it silences the reasoning in us that would tell us not to be true to our vocation.

Faith is often naked, deprived of support in human reasoning or in feelings of consolation. This means that our vocation can seem completely pointless. What is the "use", for example, of devoting oneself to the care of a sick or senile relative? Why not let the state take over? What is the "use" of maintaining parochial structures for a handful of Catholics in the Scandinavian diaspora – why not employ the priests more "efficiently" elsewhere? (When I told a priest friend in Latin America that I was to take up a post in Norway, he wrote that I was going to "a luxury Church" and that I should come where priests were "needed"...)

What is the "use" of remaining with a marriage partner who is unfaithful? Why acquiesce in the pain caused by a transfer from one religious house to another, or by difficult members of one's community?

More and more, I come to sense that hanging on in difficult situations where God calls us to live – even when it seems quite pointless to do so – is a very fundamental virtue. I think this has something to do with the fundamental bodiliness of the human person: the basic fact about my being in church at prayer is the bodily fact of my presence, which is the essential foundation on which God can build something for his kingdom, and even if my thoughts and feelings are far from him, yet the very fact of my bodily presence in his house is positive, in that it at least opens a door for him. In the same way, the simple and perhaps undramatic faithfulness of getting from one day to the next, praying always for the strength to get through the next half-hour or the next few hours, seems to me profoundly important. It establishes the essential foundation of stability on which God can build something for his kingdom.

I have mentioned in an earlier chapter the pervasive temptation today in married life, in religious houses and seminaries to get out, to go away, to give up the fight even when the problems are slight (at least in the eyes of an outsider). Here it is important to appreciate the value of sheer hanging on, whatever one's reason and emotions say. Two stories from the desert fathers make this point.

"A brother was oppressed by the temptation to leave the monastery. He went and told his abbot about this. The abbot said: 'Go and sit in your cell and entrust your body as a pledge to the walls of the cell. Do not go out of it – let your imagination think whatever it wants, only do not allow your body to leave the cell!'"

Such a strategy completely undercuts the tyranny of the reason and the emotions, by hanging on physically to the vocation. Another strategy is found in another story:

"One brother spent nine years in the struggle against the

temptation to leave the monastery. Every morning he got his cloak ready for his departure, and when the evening came he said to himself, 'Tomorrow I am going to leave here.' In the morning he would say, 'Let us try to hold out again today, for the sake of the Lord.' When he had done this for nine years, God took all the temptation from him, and he was at peace."

These strategies of hanging on "for the Lord's sake" are certainly not easy to put into practice. Widespread ideas of what authenticity and spontaneity in our conduct mean incline us to act upon our reasonings and/or our emotions (depending on what kind of person one happens to be, one swayed more by thinking or more by feeling). But true authenticity means being and becoming the person that *God* wants me to be and become, receiving myself from his hands as a gift. And precisely because this means a process of growth, and growth inevitably means crisis and pain, one must hang on, "hoping against hope" if need be. Those who are tempted to give up ought to be encouraged to meditate on each phrase of these two stories from the desert. They contain acute psychological and theological insight.

These strategies may be unglamorous and undramatic, but they can save lives.

Jeremiah hangs on, and the Lord delivers him in due time. The "fire" is decisive for him in his response to the temptation to abandon his calling. If we are willing to hang on, in spite of the pain, we too shall be delivered – the nine years of the brother in the second story are a reminder that this can take time.

* * *

A second point is that one can praise God in the depths, *without* robbing these depths of their seriousness.

A superficial understanding of thanksgiving often seems to neutralise suffering in a way that is deeply un-human. I recall a "testimony" once at a prayer group in which the speaker said enthusiastically ("gushed" might be the more appropriate word), "Yes, if my car breaks down in the middle of the countryside, miles from the nearest petrol station, I ought just to say, 'Thank you, Jesus!'" Apart from the question why I should thank *Jesus* for something that would presumably be my own fault, for having neglected to fill up the tank of my car, I have never grasped why one should want to give *thanks* for such an inconvenience. And ought I also to give him thanks if I discover that I have cancer? Ought I to tell parents to thank Jesus that their teenage son is addicted to heroin? There is something here that is reminiscent of Mary Baker Eddy's denial of the reality of suffering; the whole problem with Christian Science, of course, being that suffering does unfortunately exist.

I fear that the same criticism can be made of a well-meant rubric which allows funeral Masses to be celebrated in white vestments. The idea is that the ritual marking a Christian death is always a celebration of the mystery of the resurrection of Jesus. This is true, but only on the theological, intellectual plane. It simply obliterates the *emotional truth,* expressed by the black or violet vestments, that we mourn the dead. The emotional message expressed by white vestments is that we are glad that this person is dead! No matter how firm our belief in the resurrection, our human grief at a death is a truth that has the right to be expressed. Indeed, if we cannot express the emotional truth of our sorrow, we shall find that we *as a community*, as the publicly visible Catholic Church, stop taking death and bereavement, separation and loss and destruction, with the proper seriousness. There are already many signs of this, as when funerals are held privately, and the widowed in a parish are virtually shunned by their embarrassed acquaintances. But if death is no longer allowed in public to be the terrible thing it is, we shall find that we no longer know how to express in public our paschal faith in the resurrection of Jesus as the hope of liberation from death for ourselves and for those we love.

Both truths must be held together, without attempting to dissolve the tension in such a way that one is suppressed in favour of the other, in the same way that thanksgiving and despair coexist in Jeremiah. This is exceedingly difficult. Like the "hanging on" of which I have spoken, it is possible only where a deep faith exists, deeper than either reasoning or emotions and capable of integrating both. Suffering is a reality that can fill the whole horizon of human life and penetrate every fibre of a person; and yet "the light shines in the darkness, and the darkness has not mastered it" (Jn 1:5).

These words are so familiar that we may fail to notice how odd they are. If we light a candle or switch on an electric light, the darkness disappears. Even if we light up only a corner of the room, we would still say that there is an area of light and an area of darkness, perhaps separated by imprecise borders. But the prologue to John's Gospel says that light and darkness coexist: the light is "in the darkness" and shines there, while the darkness tries to take hold of it, to overcome it, but does not succeed. The light is stronger, because this light is Jesus himself, and the light will ultimately win. But at present, our life is a constant dialogue between light and darkness. There is no place for superficial optimism in the Johannine prologue, no attempt to dissolve the logical tensions – indeed, we have the exact opposite of any such attempt in the fourth Gospel, which identifies Jesus' "glory" with his suffering on the Cross, without either neutralising the brutality of his suffering or diminishing the omnipotence of his glory.

The story of Jesus shows us that suffering and death are utterly real. At the same time, it shows us that not they, but resurrection and life, have the final word. We believe also that "Christ leads me through no darker rooms than he went through before" (in the words of Richard Baxter's hymn). This means that all our suffering is already present in his. He could not experience every individual form of human suffering – he did not die of cancer or have a child addicted to heroin. But in his suffering, every pain that we can know is given a place. Archbishop Anthony Bloom once said that when the Russian Orthodox Church lost the Christ of its splendid cathedrals in the aftermath of the October Revolution, it discovered that, wherever it came in its humiliation and degradation, he had been there before as "the Christ of the concentration camps".

* * *

Even this can sound somewhat too "spiritual". It needs concrete testimonies like that of Cardinal Jozef Slipyi (+ 1984) to bring it down to earth. In the years he spent in exile in the West, he spoke movingly of the sheer harshness and unglamorousness of life in a Soviet prison camp, knowing all the time how easy it would be to get out of it all if he had abandoned communion with the Catholic Church – in other words, if he abandoned his faithfulness to a vocation that had led to such suffering.

A superficial kind of hagiography has often underestimated the psychological suffering that is involved in the fidelity to one's vocation. A case in point is Benedetta Bianchi Porro (1936-1964).

The facts of her life are extraordinary enough in themselves. As a twenty-year-old medical student at the University of Milan, she diagnosed her own condition as an incurable diffused neurofibromatosis which led to a state of total helplessness: completely deaf, blind, paralysed, incontinent, without the senses of taste or smell, her only means of contact with the external world was the palm of her right hand, on which her mother tapped out letters of the alphabet, "reading" books and letters to her in this way. She was able to speak. A hopeless invalid, humanly speaking, utterly dependent on others: but a woman who gave

71

life to others, dictating letters and animating a circle of young people who gathered round her bed.

It is scarcely surprising that the hagiographers got to work on her and transformed her into a creature of a rather cloying sweetness and light (as they did earlier with St Thérèse of Lisieux, whose authentic figure disappeared under a shower of roses). I knew only this kind of account of Benedetta, and I was disconcerted when I read Lorenzo da Fara's 1986 biography of her, which shows how she grew into the acceptance of her condition as something positive, as her specific vocation, *in the literal and emotional darkness* which defined the boundaries of her life. I was disconcerted to read of her psychological difficulties, of the crisis provoked by her blindness (which became final in the course of the celebration of Mass in her hospital room), and of the petulance she could show even at the end of her life. On the last Sunday before her death, none of her friends had come to see her, and she became very depressed. Her mother tried to cheer her up by saying, "But I am here, Benedetta." The only reply was: "But you are always here, mamma!" (She later apologised.) This is not very "edifying", not the kind of thing one looks for in saints' biographies. But I came to see that the greatness of Benedetta Bianchi Porro, who was able to ask her mother on the last night of her life to kneel down beside her bed and thank God "for everything that he has given me... for he who is mighty has done great things in me", is not in the least contradicted by the evidence of her human reactions to an immense weight of suffering. On the contrary, such reactions are *the darkness in which the light shines.* And the light is stronger than the darkness. In her humanity, which did not gloss over the horrendous suffering with a trivial "Thank you, Jesus!", but reacted *normally* to it, God found a space in which he could work. She hung on faithfully, instead of rejecting his call, and so she entered upon a wholly unforeseeable ministry to others. Right to the close of her life there is a discernible growth in God's possession of her, in the victory of light over darkness. She had wanted to help other people by becoming a doctor; through her faithfulness when this hope was crushed, the light shone in her for many people, and has continued to shine after her death.

Benedetta's vocation and her charism were individual, like those of all Christians; we who tread a less exposed path can learn from her to praise and thank God in our doubts, in our depression, in our temptations to infidelity to his call, knowing in faith that the light shines in *our* darkness too, for others and also for ourselves.

* * *

If we have grasped this truth about our relationship to God, it ought to be easier for us to show compassion, i.e. to "suffer with" others. Benedetta Bianchi Porro defined love as *"living in other people's suffering"*. This must always be our attitude as Christians, and it is possible only if we ourselves have confronted the depths in our own pain and loss and have found Christ there as "light in the darkness".

Otherwise, despite all our fine words about solidarity and all the good and important causes we give our money to, our attitude to the poor and the suffering will in reality only be that described by Hervé Guibert in his novel "A l'ami qui ne m'a pas sauvé la vie": "The nurse who was to take my blood test looked at me with a gaze full of sweetness (*douceur*) which meant: 'You are going to die before me'."

Benedetta's words are frightening. But are not Guibert's words even more frightening? We ourselves must choose which formulation is to be incarnated in our lives.

* * *

We can sum up this chapter, which has reflected on something of the difficulty of fidelity to one's vocation, by saying that we have no need to "edify" God when we pray

73

to him. Nor do we need to strike poses in order to edify other people (or even to edify ourselves). Our fear, our anguish, our despair, our hopelessness, our anger: all of these can have a place in our prayer, for we need not be afraid of shocking God. We come before him as we are, wounded and inglorious, but called by him to serve him and build up his kingdom. And because his light in us will ultimately overcome the darkness, all the negative emotions can – and must – find their place in our dialogue of love with the Lord. By bringing them to him, we bring ourselves to him in the fullness of our reality, offering him not just the pious bit of ourselves, but the whole of ourselves as the space in which he can work and bring about in us whatever *he* wills, the vocation to which he has called us in a wholly individual manner from all eternity.

VII

His strength in our weakness

The title of this chapter is taken from the words of the Lord to St Paul, "My grace is enough for you: for power is made perfect in weakness" (2 Cor 12:9). The full depth of this truth can be disclosed only in the New Testament, where we see the decisive victory of God in the utter powerlessness of the death on the Cross, and where we then see how vocation for the Christian means entering into precisely this mystery of the Cross. In this chapter, we shall see how this theme is foreshadowed in the old covenant.

God called Moses, who was incapable of speaking, to lead his people out of Egypt. He called Samuel while still a child to begin his prophetic ministry (cf. 1 Sam 3). He called Amos, who was "no prophet, nor a prophet's son, but a herdsman, and a dresser of sycamore trees" (7:14) to proclaim his word to Israel. As we have seen in the previous chapter, he called the young and inexperienced Jeremiah to prophesy to Jerusalem. But the most important foreshadowing of the victory which he will one day win through the weakness of the Cross comes in his call of David through the prophet Samuel (1 Sam 16). Here the disparity between the immensity of the task and the littleness of the human means available is seen in an especially dramatic and vivid manner.

The background to this calling is God's rejection of Saul, the first king of his people, because of his disobedience. Samuel is told to go to Bethlehem and anoint one of the sons of Jesse as Saul's successor. We must note here that Saul was an exceptional figure: we read in the narrative of his call that "when he took his stand among the people, he was head and shoulders taller than any of them"

(1 Sam 10:23); in other words, just the man to lead a people in battle, one whose commanding height would be a great help to his troops in the mêlée. When Samuel comes to the house of Jesse, he applies the same criterion, that of the outward physical appearance: "he looked on Eliab and thought, 'Surely the Lord's anointed is now before him'" (16:6). But the Lord does not accept Eliab, Jesse's eldest son, telling Samuel, "Do not look on *his appearance or on the height of his stature,* because I have rejected him; for the Lord does not see as mortals see; they look on the outward appearance, but the Lord looks on the heart." And the Lord rejects all seven of Jesse's sons – that is to say, those seven sons whom Jesse had thought it worthwhile to present to the prophet. For Jesse too is guided by the external appearance of the sons whom he "makes pass before Samuel".

"Samuel said to Jesse, 'Are all your sons here?' And he said, 'There remains yet the youngest, but he is keeping the sheep.' And Samuel said to Jesse, 'Send and bring him; for we will not sit down until he comes here.' He sent and brought him in. Now he was ruddy, and had beautiful eyes, and was handsome. The Lord said, 'Rise and anoint him; for *this* is the one.'"

Our mental picture of David is almost sure to be influenced by the genius of Michelangelo's "David" in Florence – a vigorous young man well able to fight battles, one who could doubtless answer the prophet Samuel's search for a new king in Israel. The figure of the biblical story itself is quite different. Unlike his eldest brother Eliab, who did inspire this reaction in Samuel, David is shown as one who was not worthy to be presented to the prophet or to be a soldier in Saul's army, and was fit only to look after the sheep ("those few sheep in the wilderness", as his warrior brother Eliab sneers later, 17:28). There is nothing about his outward appearance to suggest that he would make a good leader in war; indeed, the reference to his "beautiful eyes" and his "handsomeness" suggests a young man with a distinctly effeminate appearance. If we put Michelangelo's statue out of our minds and simply read the text of 1 Samuel, we cannot explain why God should say: "This is the one!"

The perplexity increases in the following chapter, when it is David who is to engage the Philistine champion Goliath in single combat. Goliath is a mountain of a man whose immense size and strength are portrayed graphically. His height was "six cubits and a span"; his coat weighted "five thousand shekels of bronze"; "the shaft of his spear was like a weaver's beam, and his spear's head weighed six hundred shekels of iron" (17:4ff). Against this giant, what can David achieve? He cannot even bear the weight of King Saul's armour.

The odds against David seem overwhelming. Indeed, we may presume that the only reason why Saul and his army allowed someone so ludicrously ill-fitted as David to engage Goliath in single combat was precisely the *absolute hopelessness* of their situation: since they were bound to lose such a combat anyway, what did it matter whether their champion was a "mighty man of valour" or merely a boy like David?

But perhaps the sheer impossibility here, the deliberate exaggeration in the superhuman dimensions of Goliath, may remind us of an earlier "sheer impossibility" in salvation history. It was out of the question for a ninety-year-old woman to give birth, yet Sarah bore Isaac, the son of the promise, *because God was faithful.* It is out of the question for David to win – "You are not able to go against this Philistine to fight with him," says Saul, "for you are just a boy, and he has been a warrior from his youth" – yet David kills Goliath, *because God is faithful.* The real combat is fought out on the divine level, between the Lord and the gods of the Philistines. The latter certainly seem much more powerful, because their champion Goliath is so much bigger than David, but the Lord has committed himself to his people and will therefore deliver them:

"When the Philistine looked and saw David, he disdained him, for he was only a youth, ruddy and handsome in appearance... And the Philistine *cursed David by his gods*... But David said to the Philistine, 'You come to me with sword and spear and javelin; but I come to you *in the name of the Lord of hosts, the God of the armies of Israel,* whom you have defied. This very day the Lord will deliver you into my hand... so that all the earth may know that there is a God in Israel, and that all this assembly may know that the Lord does not save by sword and spear; for the battle is the Lord's and he will give you into our hand'" (17:42ff).

"The battle is the Lord's": once again, we see that in salvation history the human actors are carrying out the work of God, who is the true actor at work in their ministry. David's utter inadequacy to carry out the task assigned him makes it completely clear that it is the Lord who saves. "In the sight of Heaven" (a reverential way of saying, "in the sight of God") "there is no difference between saving by many or by few. It is not on the size of the army that victory in battle depends, but strength comes from Heaven" (1 Macc 3:18f). These words of Judas Maccabeus state the same conviction as David's words in 1 Sam 17. The same lesson is taught by the figure of the widow Judith, the defenceless woman through whom God delivers Israel in a situation where no soldier can help, or by Gideon who is told by God to send away most of his army, for "Israel would only take the credit away from me, saying, 'My own hand has delivered me'" (Judges 7:2). Out of the original army of thirty-two thousand, a mere three hundred remain, yet God gives Israel the victory against the colossal might of Midian through these three hundred. God shows his infinite power through weak human instruments. What does this mean for us whom he calls to do his work today?

* * *

One obstacle to God's work in us can be our pride: we want to do great things for God, and we find it difficult to accept that it is he who must be thanked and praised for whatever we may have achieved. But there is another obstacle that can be equally strong: confronted (perhaps very painfully) with the evidence of our weakness, our incapacity, and even our sin, we become so obsessed by our own rottenness that we forget who it is that has called us, and who it is that is working *in* our brokenness to build up his kingdom.

Each of these reactions puts myself squarely in the centre of my perception of my vocation and ministry, and that is a place where I do not belong. Since the first danger, pride, is probably the more obviously wrong, it is worth looking more closely at the second danger, depression and resignation. The roots of this are in themselves healthy: an awareness of my own limitations and of my sinfulness is good in checking at the roots any tendency to self-congratulation. But this can get out of hand. Such an awareness is meant to dispossess me of my own life and hand it over to the Lord, so that *he* can take the responsibility for what I do in his service – it is not meant to become the sole horizon of my existence.

Carried to extremes, this attitude can lead us to doubt the reality of God's forgiveness of our sins. The diary of Blessed Faustina Kowalska (+ 1938) relates how one of the elderly sisters in her convent told her with tears that she believed all her sacramental confessions had been made badly and that she doubted whether Jesus had forgiven her sins. She asked Sister Faustina to pray for her, and Faustina received this reply from the Lord: "Tell her that her lack of trust wounds my heart more than the sins she has committed." The elderly nun heard these words with great joy; I have told this story many times to people who feared that their sins were too great to be forgiven by God, and I have sensed the same joy in them too.

Trust is born of faith in the God whose nature (as the

Anglican liturgy says) "is always to have mercy". We have indeed no reason to put faith in ourselves – the experience of temptation and of sin is too real for that. But we have every reason to put faith in the mercy of the one who has called us. This is why St Paul can say, "I do not judge myself" (1 Cor 4:3). The words in the next verse, "I am not aware of any fault that could be laid to my charge", show that Paul does examine his conscience; he does not intend to encourage the Corinthians to regard their sins lightly! No, it is because he is so keenly aware that "the one who judges me is *the Lord*" (4:4) that he can abstain from evaluating his own progress. This attitude delivers him both from pride and from depression. One of the important aspects of the act of sacramental confession is this same handing-over to the divine judge of all that I have done; I myself can be relatively unconcerned about the precise grade of seriousness (mortal or venial sin, or simply human weakness), because "the one who judges me is the Lord" and his nature "is always to have mercy". I shall say more in a later chapter about the role of the sacrament of confession in the life of the one who is called. Here I note only the self-effacement, the dispossession, involved in withdrawing my life from my own judgment and submitting it to God's judgment in the sacrament.

* * *

Chapter 68 of the Rule of St Benedict deals with the problem of the monk who is commanded to do something "impossible". Benedict tells him that, if he fails to convince his superior that the command truly is impossible, "he should obey, in love and trusting in the help of God". This is the response of a David or a Gideon, who are called to be God's instruments in hopeless situations.

God can indeed call us to do impossible things. My monastery in Italy was next door to the generalate of the Sisters of Jesus the Redeemer, who were founded in the last century by Victorine Le Dieu. This woman spent most of her life writing Rules and getting permission from civil and religious authorities to open houses for non-existent nuns: the few who did join her left her, and at her death in 1884 she was in fact the only member of her Institute. It was apparently impossible for her to carry out what she perceived to be her vocation in the Church. Nevertheless, she persevered up to her death. On her deathbed she was looked after by a young woman who then felt called to take the habit of the Institute and to carry it on, and today it is a large international congregation with a ministry of various apostolic works rooted in eucharistic adoration – precisely the combination that her contemporaries thought "crazy".

Humanly speaking, her biography is a depressing book. Every time she seems to be getting off the ground, her Institute collapses around her, and we see the seventy-five-year old foundress waiting once again for hours at a time in the antechambers of Italian bureaucrats and being told by priests that there is no room for her charism in the Church. But her story can simultaneously be read at a deeper level, where we can affirm that she paid the price of the subsequent flowering in her own painful life, "in love and trusting in the help of God".

It is easy, when one sees the fruit of her fidelity to a seemingly "impossible" calling, to see the point of all that Victorine Le Dieu went through. But (as with the martyrs of whom I spoke in chapter IV) she herself could not know what the outcome would be after her own death! She could not be sure of the authenticity of her charism, nor – supposing that it was in fact authentic – that others in the Church would respond positively to it. She had to hang on without ever seeing any fruit of her struggles. This is not an easy option. It is a great deal more logical to abandon such a vocation. But because the work was God's, the single grain buried in the earth brought forth much fruit (cf. Jn 12:24).

* * *

"My grace is enough for you: for power is made perfect in weakness" – divine power *in* human weakness. Most of us are not called to be founders, or to win physical battles like St Joan of Arc (+ 1431). But every disciple whom the Lord calls to serve him is in fact called to do something that is impossible for human means alone. We are always David facing Goliath, whatever the concrete circumstances of our lives may be. It is important that we remember David's reply to the Philistine champion: "The battle is the Lord's, and he will give you into our hand". He does not leave us to fight unaided, for it is in our weakness that his power comes to full effect.

The only truly potent obstacle to the Lord's power is our concentration on ourselves – either in a pride that attributes the victory to our own selves, or in a resignation that says we are too weak for him to do anything in us. But if we look to him, to the one who calls us and sustains us, he will give us the victory in the way and at the time that he determines.

Part II

IN THE NEW COVENANT

VIII
God calls Mary

Salvation history in the Old Testament begins with the calling of Abram. Salvation history in the New Testament begins with the calling of Mary. The structure of the story is the same as the structure of the stories in the Old Testament: God calls a person in her unrepeatable historical circumstances to say "yes" to him and thus to open up a space where he can work. And just as those whose vocations we have seen in the first part of this book were called to ministries that surpassed their human capabilities, so Mary is called to a ministry that is utterly impossible without the divine initiative: she is to be the virgin mother of the Redeemer.

Isaac, Samson, Samuel, John the Baptist: all are born contrary to human expectation, but at least we can say that all are conceived and born in the normal way. "There is for all *one* entrance into life," says the Book of Wisdom (7:6). But this is not to be the case with the Son of God: "The Holy Spirit will come upon you," says the angel to Mary in Nazareth, "and the power of the Most High will overshadow you. Therefore the holy child that is born will be called the Son of God" (Lk 1:35). Mary's virginity must be her free choice: "I do not know a man" (1:34), creating the possibility for the Holy Spirit to act in this way.

We can miss the radical newness of Mary's virginity because we, as Christians, have a long tradition of the positive evaluation of virginity. Virginity was important for the world in which Jesus was born only as a precondition of marriage, as a proof that the husband would be the first man to "possess" his bride: this is the point of the prescriptions in Deut 22 about the "tokens of virginity" which the parents of the bride could show as proof that their daughter had been a virgin on the day of her wedding. Virginity in itself was not an option that could be chosen – even if a woman had been free to decide about her own life, instead of being married off by her family – because it had no religious value within Judaism.

I did once hear a sermon about the temple in Jerusalem which mentioned "the quarters of the temple virgins", but this is a Roman idea – the Vestal virgins who guarded the sacred fire – found, not in any Jewish document, but in a second-century Christian text, the Protevangelium of James. We see the classical Jewish evaluation of virginity in the story of Jephthah's daughter (Judges 11). He vows that he will offer as a burnt offering the first who crosses the threshold of his house on his return from victory over the Ammonites: and this is his only daughter. She acquiesces in his vow, but says, "Let this thing be done for me: Grant me two months, so that I may go and wander on the mountains, and bewail my virginity, my companions and I" (11:37). When she returns, he kills her, and the author underlines the tragedy of the story by saying, "She had never slept with a man. So there arose an Israelite custom that for four days every year the daughters of Israel would go out to lament the daughter of Jephthah the Gileadite." We know from Jewish documents that this tradition continued into the New Testament period, and the Chronicle of Jerahmeel gives the text of her lament:

"I have not looked out from beneath my bridal canopy,
and my wedding crown is not finished.
And I have not put on the fair adornments
of the bride who sits in her woman's quarters.
I have not been perfumed with myrrh and fragrant aloes,
nor have I been anointed with the oil of anointing
which is made ready for me.
Alas, my mother, in vain have you given birth to me.
See your only daughter – her bridal canopy is in Sheol..."

I have quoted this text as the background against which we must see the virginity of Our Lady. Jephthah's daughter, in this lament written in the first century of the Christian era, can say to her mother, "In vain have you given birth to me", because she is to die a virgin – it is a life wasted. Her death itself may perhaps have some religious value, in the sense that it is the fulfilment of her father's vow to God, but her virginity as such is utterly useless. Indeed, had it been freely chosen, it could have been seen as disobedience of the Creator's command, "Be fruitful and multiply" (Gen 1:28).

Mary's virginity marks a border between the two covenants. The first creation, in which marriage and the procreation of children were the religious norm, is superseded by the new creation in which two things happen: marriage is raised to the dignity of a sacrament, one of the seven pillars on which the house of the Lord is built, and virginity is consecrated as a positive gift of self to God. We see in the calling of Mary a wholly new act of God, not prepared by anything he had done in the old covenant.

Were Mary to be "only" a virgin (so to speak), we should have to see consecrated virginity and celibacy within Christianity primarily in terms of sacrifice, of what one "gives up"; and of course, this is how Christian celibacy and virginity have in fact very often been presented – in negative terms. (For example, the usual German word for consecrated celibacy is "Ehelosigkeit", which literally means "marriagelessness": the word itself denotes a *lack of something*.) But this is only one side of the picture. In her virginity, Mary is called to be a mother, and this opens up for the Church the possibility that consecrated celibacy can be fruitful in a way analogous to the sacrament of matrimony. St Paul can call himself both the father and the mother of his communities: "Even if you have a myriad of teachers in Christ, you do not have many fathers: for it was I who begot you in Christ Jesus through the gospel" (1 Cor 4:15); "My children, for whom I suffer birthpangs afresh, until Christ takes form in you!" (Gal 4:19).

Thus virginity, in Christian terms, is not the dead end that it was for Jephthah's daughter. To see it (or attempt to live it) only as a sacrifice, only as something deficient ("marriagelessness"), is to miss the whole point. We are not called to assume a crushing load of sacrifice: we are called to offer ourselves to the Lord so that through us, others may be born for him. Those who renounce biological children "for my sake and for the sake of the gospel" are not promised solely suffering and frustration: they are promised "children, now in this time", because "what is impossible for human beings is possible for God, for everything is possible for God" (Mk 10:27ff).

These words take us back to Gabriel's final words to Mary: "For nothing shall be impossible for God" (Lk 1:37). The fruitfulness of our life has its origin in the fruitfulness of her life. And this, at the deepest level, is why the Church proclaims Mary (who was not a nun, but – sociologically speaking – a housewife) model of the consecrated life. In her, we see by analogy the creative potential for God in a way of life which, humanly speaking, cannot be fruitful.

* * *

Interviewers like provocative questions. They hope for a revealing answer, perhaps even an indiscreet answer, that will be more interesting for their readers. I recently read three very interesting interviews with members of a German Protestant community, the Jesus Brotherhood, in which each brother was asked the question – provocative in the context of the Lutheran tradition with its clear rejection of monasticism, especially for men – "Why did you enter a religious community?" The first said that he had entered because he wanted to work with young people, the second that he wanted to proclaim the Word of God. Each of these is a very worthy aim in life, but I thought that it was only the third who gave an answer that was genuinely capable of supporting a whole life in celibacy: "Aus Liebe zu Jesus – out of love for Jesus."

This formulation may sound rather too pious. But in the end, is there any other motivation for the religious life or the diocesan priesthood that will enable me to commit the whole of myself to such a ministry for the whole of my life? Working with young people and proclaiming the Word of God are not motivations that commit me on such a deep existential level; by themselves, they neither require nor adequately support a celibate lifestyle, and we see plenty of married Christians of both sexes who exercise these ministries, and exercise them very well. The argument about the greater "availability" of a celibate priest to his flock is often heard, not least on the lips of the Pope and the bishops. But this is a worldly argument which uses the criterion of efficiency to justify something that cannot be justified in this way: for even if it could be shown that the average celibate priest is in fact more available than the average married minister of another Church, that would be only the *fruit* of his celibacy, never the motivation for it. Celibacy makes sense only "out of love for Jesus".

This love takes on an exclusive character, analogous to the love of one single partner in marriage, which makes it impossible *for me* to marry: I become what tradition calls a "bride of Christ". There may be psychological hurdles to be overcome before a man can see himself in this light! But it is not the word "bride" that counts. It is the reality of the consecration of the whole of my being in love to Jesus Christ, in a way that rules out my consecrating myself in love to another person.

This has nothing to do with a negative view of marriage or sexuality. It is not a claim that a life in celibacy is "better". (Paul does claim this at 1 Cor 7:38, and the Catholic tradition has followed him in this, but the Church's understanding of marriage and family life has developed so radically in this century that no one would take this position seriously today.) All are called to love Christ. Some consecrate themselves to him through the sacrament of matrimony, and some find that the relationship of love to him takes up so much space that they must expose themselves utterly to him in consecrated celibacy.

We are often afraid to speak in these terms. But this is the only credible framework in which Christian celibacy can be lived as something fruitful for myself and for the whole Church. Only a life built on love will carry me through the inevitable suffering, and give meaning to a sacrifice which is sheerly incomprehensible without that love.

I once had a conversation with a Muslim in St Peter's Square in Rome. He had seen my religious habit and asked if I was a Catholic priest. When I said that I was, he asked me point-blank, "But how can you live without sex?" He might just possibly have understood me, if I had spoken about "availability" or about working with youth and proclaiming the Word of God. He had no possibility of understanding the only answer I myself consider correct, namely "Out of love for Jesus". It is tragic that so many in the Church, even among those who so loudly defend priestly celibacy, are apparently in the same situation as the Muslim I met: personal love for the living person of Jesus Christ seems to come very far down the list of their priorities, if they mention it at all! But it is doubtless safer to ensconce oneself behind talk of pastoral efficiency, or to console seminarians with assurances that "the next Pope" will change the Church's discipline (something that has been said for as long as I can remember!), than to dare to speak of Jesus Christ and of love for him...

* * *

We see in the story of Mary's call this quality of total love, of total self-giving: "Behold the servant of the Lord: let it happen to me as you have said" (Lk 1:38). We see here a person who is empty of herself, who claims nothing for herself, who does not seek to make decisions about how her future life is to run: "Let it happen to me as *you* have said". We shall return in the next chapter to the word "servant", which is the key to Mary's vocation. Let us end this chapter by reflecting on her final words to the angel Gabriel.

It is obvious enough what is renounced by the vows of poverty and chastity. What does the vow of obedience renounce, exactly? We can say that this vow treads in Mary's footsteps by renouncing the right to determine one's own future. And this is a fundamental matter. No matter how circumscribed my possibilities of self-realisation may be in concrete fact, I can at least nourish dreams and hopes. Mary renounces any such dreams and hopes of her own, in favour of God's free disposal over her life.

This is the renunciation involved in the incarnation itself. "My food is to do the will of the one who sent me, and to accomplish his work," says Jesus (Jn 4:34), living this renunciation to its uttermost consequences when he prays in Gethsemane, "Not what I will, but what you will" (Mk 14:36). In theological language, Mary's act of renunciation expresses the fact that she has already been brought (through the immaculate conception) inside the sphere of the redemption which her Son is to win at a subsequent date through his obedience in his life and his death on the Cross. We who come later in time than the obedience of Jesus draw from the same spring as Mary: when we give up our own will, we do what Jesus did. This means that our obedience shares in a mysterious way in his work of redemption: like our poverty and our chastity, our vow of obedience is not to be seen primarily in terms of what it costs *us,* but of what it can mean *for others.* Mary's "yes" to her calling brings her to stand under the Cross on

Golgotha, and our "yes" will bring us there too. But this means life for the Church and for the world.

As with the other vows, we need not be surprised if God takes us literally and does in fact bring us to Golgotha. And here too, the limits of human understanding are left behind. Everyone in society has to obey. One obeys employers, one obeys the laws of the state, one obeys within family life. But there are always limits where we resist what we perceive as encroachments on our freedom; in extreme cases, we speak of basic human rights which are being trampled on. What, then, are we to say – even if we accept the principle that "the Church is not a democracy" – about the obedience exacted of founders separated from their own Institutes, like Blessed Jeanne Jugan (+ 1879), foundress of the Little Sisters of the Poor, or Father Kentenich, founder of the Schönstatt movement (+ 1965)? Is a posthumous beatification enough of a compensation for the suffering demanded by the men who had authority in the Church of Christ?

Or what of theologians? Is a cardinal's hat, conferred when its wearer has become very old like John Henry Newman (created a cardinal at the age of seventy-eight in 1879) or Yves Congar (created a cardinal at the age of ninety in 1994), compensation enough for all the suspicions cast on him in the course of his work? Part of the answer may be glimpsed in the life of the theologian Henri de Lubac (+ 1991). He was in the right, and those who silenced him were in the wrong (although they were sincerely convinced that it was their sacred obligation to act as they did). He submitted, entering the mystery of the silent Lamb of God, and his theological work survived. He became not merely a scholar, but a witness. Pope John Paul II acknowledged de Lubac not only as a theologian – he is in fact virtually the only theologian whom the Pope has quoted while he was still alive – but also as a witness, when he visited Paris and said, in his presence, "Je m'incline devant le père de Lubac – I bow my head before Father de Lubac."

When he made him a cardinal in 1983, he gave him the same "title" as the cardinal who had condemned him in the 1950's. His participation in the Cross bore fruit that enriched the Church.

This is the same fruitfulness we can see in the suffering of the martyrs, a participation in the same mystery of *faith*. Two separate questions are involved here, one concerning those called on to obey, the other concerning those who exercise authority. But the answers converge in the same direction.

This is the direction of the Cross. If, like Mary, I have said, "Let it happen to me as *you* have said", then I have handed myself over to God without reserve. I have given up any claim to the autonomous direction of my own life. God has the right (as I said when speaking of the sacrifice of Isaac) to cash my blank cheque, filling in the amount that he decides – even if that means everything I have. It might be easier to accept this, if God were to descend in a crash of thunder on the mountain and issue his demands in a ringing voice. It is much harder when he speaks through other human beings, who are certainly fallible and may even be corrupt. But it is precisely through such persons – even the corrupt – that God works, just as it was through the sin and weakness of the Jewish leaders and Pontius Pilate that Jesus came to the Cross and brought about our salvation. We must not be so afraid of dying that we refuse the Cross in the specific form in which God offers it to us. The Cross I would have chosen for myself is never the Cross that God has destined for me: and it is only *his* Cross that will bear fruit.

Those in authority in the Church, at whatever level of responsibility for others, must respect their fundamental rights. It is intolerable that they should behave dictatorially towards believers (cf. 1 Pet 5:1ff). Yet it can be the duty of those in authority – bishops or superiors, for example – to lead those under them to the Cross. It can be the superior's task, his or her contribution to the kingdom of God, to confront a person with the challenge to a costly obedience which will bear fruit for the kingdom of God in a way that surpasses human reasoning. It should not be necessary to emphasise that such a role requires very fine discernment. It is very easy to be guided by human reasoning and emotion and to confuse these with the promptings of the Holy Spirit. But it *can* be the duty of the superior, under God, to lay the Cross of Christ on the shoulders of another.

We see something of what this means in the life of Mary, whose "yes" to the Father's will for her is "cashed" at the foot of the Cross of Jesus. The example of her fruitful acceptance of this will can give us light, when we too are directed in obedience to the Cross. We shall come back to this theme in chapter X.

IX
The visitation

Gabriel's message to Mary contains the testimony provided by what has happened to her kinswoman Elizabeth: "She too has conceived a son in her old age, and this is the sixth month for her, although she was called sterile" (Lk 1:36). This too is a birth that comes from the divine initiative, as the preceding narrative in the Gospel makes clear.

Mary's first reaction to the angel's message is to "rise up" and "go with haste" to see Elizabeth. The annunciation speaks of Mary's intimate relationship to God as the mother of his Son, and the visitation speaks of her love of neighbour, which is inextricably linked to the first act whereby she gives herself to God. For as we have seen in the vocations in the old covenant, the special relationship between God and the one he calls is never something exclusively for him or her: it is always given for the sake of others. The annunciation and the visitation can therefore be seen as one single mystery in which Mary says "yes" to her call.

When Mary comes to Elizabeth's house, she does not come alone. She comes as "the mother of my Lord" (1:43), she brings Jesus with her, so that the meeting of the two women is also the meeting of their two unborn children. Later, when Jesus is born, the Gospels tell how shepherds and wise men from the east come to see him; but first, nine months before his birth, Mary brings him to Elizabeth. For this is the highest form of the love of neighbour: to bring Jesus to her. Let us once again ask the question: what does this mean for us in our own calling?

* * *

In the last chapter, I quoted St Paul's words to the Galatians: "My children, for whom I suffer birthpangs afresh, until Christ takes form in you!" (4:19). The Christian life is a process of configuration to Christ, so that he can "take form" in us. This process begins at baptism, in which we have "clothed ourselves" in Christ (cf. Gal 3:27); while baptism is a rite that cannot be repeated and thus represents a once-for-all change in our life, the command to "clothe ourselves" must be repeated again and again: "Take off the old man... and put on the new man" (Eph 4:22ff). I translate the Greek text here (*anthrôpon,* which is gender-neutral and means "human being") with the word "man", because this "new man, in accordance with God, established in the righteousness and holiness of truth", is of course Christ himself. "We are to grow in every respect into him" (4:15). At every stage of our lives, therefore, it can be affirmed that Christ has not yet fully taken form in us, that we have not yet fully clothed ourselves in him. We never reach a point in our life on earth at which we can say, "Now I have arrived". Christ is no static model, but one who always beckons us onwards, one who calls us to go ever further and further in being configured to him.

The awareness of our imperfection, the awareness that we still have a very long way to go, should generate in us a humility that will let God get to work in us. We see that we have no reason to be proud of ourselves, so we put our trust in him. But there can also be in us the reaction of an exaggerated humility, which is so taken up with the evidence of our imperfection that it *refuses* God's call to act. (I have spoken in chapter VII of a related reaction: depression and resignation in the face of one's own incapacity to do what God demands.) For example, many priests are reluctant to preach to nuns or to hear their confessions because they do not feel "expert" enough in spiritual matters, and feel that the sisters will already have heard anything they might have to say. This may be objectively the case, and not only with nuns. I have often realised that my parishioners knew far more about the things of God than I did! But if I keep silent, I have deprived God of the opportunity of speaking precisely through my broken words, through my commonplaces, through my half-understood ideas, even through my general incompetence in spiritual things. I may perhaps bore ninety-nine per cent of those who hear me, but God can still use me to touch one person in particular – and perhaps he will then use that one person to touch the ninety-nine!

This kind of reaction – "waiting until I am fully qualified" – has nothing to do with the authentic humility of the disciple. It is in fact the exact opposite of humility, for humility accepts that I am imperfect and incompetent, and trusts in the power of the Lord who calls me and can act through me. *This* reaction assumes that my imperfection and incompetence are merely temporary, and that the day will come (or at least, could come, if I took the trouble) when I would be so far in advance of the nuns in spiritual matters that I would be able, out of my own resources, to give them the nourishment they needed. To put it in visual terms: today the nuns yawn when I preach, but *one day* they will gasp in amazement at the profundity of my spiritual wisdom! And so, when God does in fact call on me to speak today, I reply, "Not yet, Lord."

Once again, there is basically a worldly tendency at work here. A student of architecture, if asked to design a house, might perfectly well reply that, while he was not capable of carrying out such a commission today, he hoped to be able to do so after passing his final examinations.

The same mentality, which is at home in the architectural school or a medical college, can make its way surreptitiously into the Church too, where it is in fact alien. Courses and examinations of all kinds flourish in the Church today, and all this is very positive in itself. The human preparation for ministry is very important – one cannot just fold one's hands and expect God to work miracles through lazy and unprepared ministers. But there is still a quantum leap between human preparation, no matter how thorough and excellent it may be, and God's action through his minister. I must study, to open up in myself areas which God can use; but whether he does use them is his business, not mine.

It is good on occasion to see the startling disjunctures between human preparation and divine act. You can work very hard on your sermon, for example, and then you are told that the really wonderful thing about the Mass was the way the sun shone through the stained-glass window while you were preaching. Or you can find yourself stepping into the breach at the last minute, preaching what you think are banalities, and then someone tells you that your sermon was just the word from the Lord that he needed to hear. In either case, one ought to thank God that he has acted through you, in sovereign freedom, making your words a vehicle for an experience of the beauty of his house, or for a word addressed specifically to a situation unknown to you personally. The oriental tradition likes to refer to Balaam's ass, through whose mouth God spoke (Num 22), as a striking image of his power to communicate his word through anyone at all, irrespective of their degree of spiritual, theological or cultural preparation.

The fear that we are insufficiently prepared can hold us back in many situations from letting God use us as his instruments. It is no reply to point to the danger of the fools who rush in where angels fear to tread, people who are excessively willing to tell everyone else what they ought to do; one does not correct this excess by an equally exaggerated caution that, in the end, amounts to indifference to other people's situations. God uses my friendships, my work relationships, and all the networks of human ties in my life from the most superficial to the most profound, if I am willing to open them up to him. I may not have a degree in psychology, I may not be fully acquainted with all the ingredients of a problematic situation, and I certainly cannot read another person's heart. But it has been my experience that God has given other people a word to say to me at decisive moments in my life, a word with a significance that went beyond anything that they themselves could have assessed intellectually. If they had hung back diffidently, that word would not have been spoken.

The image of Our Lady carrying the newly-conceived Jesus to Elizabeth is a symbol of the point I am making here. In the literal sense, Jesus was obviously not yet "formed" in her; if she had wanted to show a child to her cousin, she would have had to wait for another nine months. But Mary "hastened to a city of Judah", without putting off the act of bringing Jesus to someone who needed help. We too do not need to wait until Jesus is fully "formed" in us – for that will be the case only when we are in heaven. As long as we are on earth, we live in imperfection. But the important thing is that *Jesus lives in us,* even if his presence is as yet a tiny presence like the presence in Mary's womb here. Because Jesus is in her, she does not hesitate to set out on the long journey south, to bring him to Elizabeth and to the unborn John. So with ourselves: even if our "grasp" on the Lord (so to speak) may be very insecure, even if we know beyond doubt that we are very incompetent ministers, our "yes" to his call impels us outwards to others, to bring him to them in their need.

And like Mary, we should "hasten" on the journey.

* * *

The first part of this chapter has looked at the visitation from Mary's point of view: she brings Jesus to Elizabeth. The story can, however, be told with Jesus as the subject: for on the deeper level, it is *Jesus* who brings Mary to Elizabeth. He is the energy that powers her love of neighbour. She is the instrument which he uses to come to Elizabeth and John.

One who brings communion to the sick is in precisely the same situation as Mary here. I can say, quite correctly, "I am bringing Jesus to the sick person." But it is more accurate to say, "Jesus is using me as his vehicle to come to the sick person." I make myself available to his love. And this can be said of every form of service. He inspires me to make myself over to him in a multitude of concrete ways, so that he can speak through my words, heal through my hands, teach, intercede, console, through my activity. These actions do not cease to be my actions: I do not become a zombie controlled from outside myself. The Lord is not a puppet-master, nor a Svengali who gives us powers not truly our own. He has complete respect for my freedom, which gives him the framework *within* which he can work, in such a way that my actions can be read on the deeper level as his. Mary's "yes" to the Holy Spirit's prompting to visit Elizabeth is given in freedom. If I too freely accept his prompting in my life, I become what Blessed Elizabeth of the Trinity called "an additional humanity" for the Word made flesh, "in which he may renew the whole of his mystery". This is a rather different idea from the concept of the imitation of Christ. This concept goes much deeper: it involves handing over the whole of myself to him so that I exercise my human freedom and initiative to the full as an instrument of the divine freedom and initiative. I do not imitate Christ's life from outside him, as a pupil may imitate a teacher. Rather, it is he himself within me who "renews" in my life what was present in his own incarnate life and in the self-giving of his passion and death.

It is this dimension of all forms of Christian ministry that ought finally to dispose of our hesitations. The human dimension is never more than that of "useless servants" (Lk 17:10 – words that are in fact much too mild to be applied to ourselves, since Jesus puts them on the lips of those who "have done *all that was commanded*" them). But to stop there is to miss the full reality of every Christian vocation: the omnipotent love of God is at work in us, building up *his* kingdom through *our* activity. This is the immense dignity of all whom the Lord calls. We are to dispossess ourselves of our lives in such a way that we become fully ourselves – as God's instruments.

The experience of this reality defies merely human logic, as we see in St Paul's intricate, almost tangled phrases: "With Christ I have been crucified: it is no longer I that live, but Christ who lives in me. As for the life that I now live in the flesh, I live in the faith of the Son of God who loved me and gave himself up for me" (Gal 2:19f). Paul does not identify himself with Jesus. Paul and Jesus are distinct, and Paul's life is genuinely his own; but its deepest truth has to be expressed in sentences that have Jesus as their subject – not Paul. The phrase "faith of the Son of God" is a literal translation; one could also translate as "faith in the Son of God" (in keeping with a similar phrase used twice in verse 16), but the literal translation seems to me more probable here. It brings out the paradoxical reality of what life in Christ means. Even my faith is something that can be expressed in a sentence with Jesus as its subject! He loves in my love, he hopes in my hope, and he believes in my believing, for "it is no longer I that live, but Christ that lives in me", "renewing" in me the "mystery" of his faith in the Father who sent him to give himself up for the life of the world.

These realities are extremely difficult to put into words. This is why the image of the visitation of Our Lady can help us to perceive them. When we see Mary bringing Jesus to Elizabeth, we also see that Jesus is bringing Mary to Elizabeth. Here too, salvation history must become "my history".

* * *

The story of the visitation is recalled very frequently in Christian prayer through the "Hail Mary", and also through the canticle of Mary, the Magnificat, which is prayed every day in the Church's liturgical evening prayer. This canticle is very rich, and discloses fresh depths as it is meditated. Most recently, it has been taken up within Latin American liberation theology and is sung as "my history", as the proclamation of hope for the exploited and oppressed. Here, I should like to offer two reflections in the context of Christian vocation.

The first reflection picks up Mary's self-description: "He looks on his servant in her lowliness" (Lk 1:48). The same word is used by Mary of herself at Nazareth: "Behold the servant of the Lord: let it happen to me as you have said" (1:48). The word "servant", like the "handmaid" of older translation, denotes a person who exists, not for herself, but for another. A servant has to do what she is told, and she exists to make life easier for her master. Household servants have virtually disappeared in our society – one sees them only in the homes of the super-rich in television soap operas – but we all know the brief experience of being waited on in a restaurant. The waiter (unless we happen to know him in another context) is not a person with whom we have an equal social relationship. He exists in our eyes, not as a person in his own right, but as one who *serves* us. If he displays any emotions of his own – tiredness or stress, or even amusement – he is liable to find that those whom he is serving disapprove of this. At best, he is allowed to laugh at their jokes. No thought is taken to save him inconvenience, and he is not permitted to answer back when customers are rude. Transpose this brief experience into a lifetime of serving other people, and we are not surprised that the few who do go into domestic service today ask for very high wages. To be a servant full time is a depersonalising, demeaning existence. We can be thankful that the labour-saving devices of modern technology have wiped out such a job. And we can appreciate how strange it is, by human reckoning, that Mary should claim such a position for herself, should choose to define herself as a "servant".

102

The strangeness increases if we translate the Greek word used in Luke's Gospel, *doulê,* with its full meaning: "slavewoman". A servant does have some rights – she gets wages, she has free time to herself, she gets a holiday, and she is a full citizen before the law. A slave has none of these rights. She has no private sphere of her own in which she can be mistress of her life and do what she wants. She may demand absolutely nothing of her master, for she is his property, with no more legal rights or safeguards than his cows or sheep. She has no pension to look forward to. The only restraint on the master will be the prudent calculation that if he works her beyond a certain point of physical endurance, she will be unable to work any further, and he will have lost a valuable piece of property.

The translation of the Magnificat which we use in the Divine Office, "He looks on his servant in her lowliness", softens Mary's words very considerably, giving them a moral tone: "lowliness" suggests a quality of humility and meek submissiveness. But the Greek word used, *tapeinôsis,* is primarily a sociological word which denotes a "low social condition", at the bottom of the ladder with no rights whatsoever. To get the full shocking force of what Our Lady is saying about herself – and not in a spirit of resignation, but of exultation – we ought to translate her literally: "He looked on his slavewoman in her low social condition." And she extends to others the joy of her own experience: "He raised up those in a low social condition" (not "the lowly", suggesting "those with the moral quality of submissiveness").

We find the same word in St Paul, who is proud to call himself "slave (*doulos* in Greek) of Christ Jesus" (Rom 1:1). And he tells the Corinthians that he and his collaborators are "your slaves because of Jesus" (2 Cor 4:5). It is in accord with this that the highest title of the pope is *servus servorum Dei,* which literally means "slave of the slaves of God". For it is not only exceptional figures, a Mary and a Paul, who are called by God to be his "slaves":

103

this word is a definition of every disciple of Jesus Christ, of every follower of him who "took the form of a slave" in a slavery that went "as far as death, death on a cross" (Phil 2:7f). It is only those at the bottom of the ladder who can be "exalted". Those who think they occupy a rung some way higher up set limits on the Lord's ability to raise them.

To call oneself a "slave" like Mary and Paul is to assert that a radical expropriation has taken place. I no longer belong to myself, I have become the property of the Lord, with no "rights" that I can invoke against him, no "safeguards" to shield me from whatever he may want me to do, or from whatever he may want to do to me. I have no right to "free time", no area of my life that is outside the boundaries of my slavery and left to my own free disposition. In human terms, this is plainly intolerable. I cannot hand myself over to another person in this manner. But if God demands such a total expropriation of me, it is because he was the first to expropriate himself, by handing over his Son to me, holding nothing back for himself. My gift of self is the response to God's self-giving to me, which is always so much greater that I can never imagine that I am giving God "more" than he has given me. If his Son became my slave, then I need not be too proud to become his.

* * *

We find the radicality of this "slavery" so difficult because we are always inclined to look for compromises in our relationship with God. We set limits, we tell him that he can have "only so much" of ourselves and of our time. We are perhaps willing to be God's "servants", but talk of "slaves" sounds like plain fanaticism.

Unfortunately for us, the radicality of the Magnificat is the radicality of the whole of the Gospel. There is a double "either/or" in Mary's words: "He casts the mighty from their thrones and raises the lowly. He fills the starving with good things, sends the rich away empty" – which *takes it for granted* that there are only two classes of humanity, those who are accepted by God (those at the bottom of society and the starving) and those whom he rejects (the mighty, the rich). There is no middle ground, no grey between the black and the white. And this is typical of the message of Jesus himself: "He who is not with me is against me; and he who does not gather with me scatters" (Mt 12:30). It seems not to occur to Jesus that one of us might say, "But I am with you up to a point", or that we might be undecided. Similarly, when he says in the Sermon on the Mount, "A good tree cannot bear bad fruit nor can a bad tree bear good fruit" (Mt 7:18), he seems not to envisage the possibility of a tree that is (like the famous curate's egg) good in parts. He simply presents a stark "either/or", with the terrible warning, "Every tree that does not bear good fruit is cut down and thrown into the fire" (7:19). There is a terrifying "take it or leave it" to Jesus' teaching.

It is clear that Our Lady knows where she stands. At Nazareth she renounces control over her own destiny, and expropriates her life into the hands of God. Mary is the model of every vocation in the Church. The question for each one of us is: Where do I stand? Am I with the sheep or with the goats, with the wise virgins or with the foolish virgins? For on the last day, there is no third option, no safe uncommitted middle ground. Judgment is a razor-sharp "either/or". And judgment is not deferred to later: judgment begins today. It is today that I have to commit myself without compromises and qualifications to the Lord who has committed himself in absolute love to me.

A great deal has been written about the inability of young people today to make life-long commitments. We are told that they shy away from saying "yes" to another person for the whole of their lives, or from saying "yes" to the religious life or the priesthood for the whole of their lives. To the extent that this is correct, we are surely right to say that one of the major causes of this "inability" is the destabilising example given by those older than themselves. But where they are given examples of fidelity, as in a woman like Mother Teresa of Calcutta, they will respond. Institutes offering a watered-down religious life will die a well-deserved death. Institutes offering a radical commitment to Christ, free of compromises, will attract generous young people who will find the ideal of life-long commitment plausible and viable.

This takes us back to the question, "Where do I stand?" If such institutes of religious life or such styles of priestly living are to exist, they will exist only because *I* accept the "either/or" alternatives posed by Jesus and say "yes" to him, handing myself over to him with the total gift of a Mary or a Paul so that my life may be the space within which he can act. I cannot displace my own responsibility in this matter. I myself must decide whether I am willing to accept the Lord's call to be his "slave", to let him renew in me the mystery of the visitation of Mary in the house of Elizabeth. Our second reflection on the Magnificat needs no further words. Let each one of us reflect on "my history" and ask, "Where do I stand?"

X
Under the Cross

The "yes" we say to God in accepting his call to follow Christ leads us to the Cross. "If anyone serves me," says Jesus, "let him follow me; and where I am, there shall my servant be too" (Jn 12:26). Any Christian spirituality which would attempt to bypass the Cross, or to pitch its tent already in the resurrection, would automatically disqualify itself as a Christian spirituality. It is only by entering the death of Christ, on a Cross imposed on us and not freely chosen in accordance with our own estimates of what we could "reasonably" be expected to bear, that we can come to enter his resurrection.

This general truth has specific implications for the way we understand our own vocation. This may be a vocation specifically to suffering, as we saw in the life of Benedetta Bianchi Porro, where the Cross is identical with the calling itself. But the Cross can also take the form of being forced – through illness, age, or external circumstances outside my control – to give up my vocation and abandon a ministry to which I have consecrated my life up to now. Rightly understood, this can be a call by God to deepen and broaden my consecration to him, to receive from him a new vocation in place of the first.

We see this illustrated in the story of Mary. Luke tells us how Mary and Joseph bring Jesus to the temple, forty days after his birth, to consecrate him to the Father (2:22ff). Simeon, inspired by the Spirit, prophesies that this child – although he is a "light for revelation to the Gentiles and for glory to your people Israel" – will be rejected. He will be "a sign that is spoken against". These words are mysterious in the extreme, if we try to hear them in their context in the

Gospel. Everything hitherto has been triumphant, with angels proclaiming the birth of Jesus and shepherds coming to venerate him. But now a completely new note is sounded, one that points forward to the passion and death of the newborn child.

With hindsight after the resurrection, we can see that there is no contradiction between the light and beauty of the stories of Jesus' birth and the darkness and blood of his death, for it is precisely on the Cross, in his supreme act of self-giving, that he is "the glory of your people Israel". But in the context of the presentation in the temple, the words of Simeon prophesying the rejection of Jesus cannot be understood. But since they are spoken on such an occasion, they cannot be dismissed. They are somehow programmatic for the future life of this child, and they are not forgotten: "his mother kept all these things in her heart," says Luke (2:51), summing up the whole of his infancy narrative in chapters 1 and 2.

Humanly speaking, Mary had good reason to remember the sombre prophecy of Simeon, for it includes her own self: "and a sword will pierce your soul too" (2:35). These words associate Mary with the destiny of her child; she too will suffer when he suffers. But this too is an incomprehensible prophecy, to be kept in her heart until its meaning is disclosed.

Mary plays no role in the public ministry of Jesus. She is present at his first miracle, when she draws to his attention the fact that the wine for the wedding feast has run out, and he changes a stupendous quantity of water into wine (Jn 2:1ff). But after this, she fades from the picture. When she tries to get access to Jesus, she is not welcomed: "While he was still speaking to the crowds, behold, his mother and his brothers stood outside and sought to speak to him. But he said to the one who told him this, 'Who is my mother, and who are my brothers?' And stretching out his hand to his disciples, he said, 'Behold my mother and my brothers! For whoever does the will of my Father who is in heaven –

this is the one who is my brother and sister and mother'"
(Mt 12:46ff). Jesus is not rejecting his mother as a person,
nor repudiating her relationship to him. He is simply pointing out that we must do the will of the Father, not our own:
it is not appropriate for Mary to take the initiative and come
to see her Son, as if their relationship were to be merely
that of a human family's love and concern. She is to come
to Jesus *when God wants this*. Her motherhood is to be that
of an exemplary disciple who waits upon the divine command before she acts. Mary learns this lesson. She withdraws to Nazareth and waits until her divine vocation brings
her once again into the presence of Jesus. This happens at
the very end of his human life, on Golgotha.

* * *

When Mary stands under the Cross of Jesus, we are not
meant to see primarily a mother's compassion with her
suffering son, as in the *Stabat Mater* and so many other
hymns and paintings. This element is there, of course, and
it is not to be devalued, as if she were merely a stoical
witness untouched by grief. But what we see first of all is
her obedience to her vocation, as Simeon had formulated it.
She stands under the Cross because God has given her the
charge to stand there. The initiative is taken by God, not by
her own maternal feelings. If we forget this point, we shall
not see the significance of the scene for ourselves as persons who are called by the Father to follow his Son.

Mary has received her motherhood as an absolute gift
from God: her only cooperation is the "yes" she said to his
call. But in her, as in all whom God calls to serve him, the
initial "yes" must be deepened, and this happens three
times in the Gospels, when she is obliged to redefine her
motherhood. The first time is when the twelve-year-old
Jesus stays behind in the temple at Jerusalem (Lk 2:41ff);
the second time is the scene from Matthew 12 quoted in the
preceding section of this chapter. Without wishing to paint

a sentimental picture, we can still sense something of the cost of such a redefinition. All parents have to learn that their children do not "belong" to them; at some point, they must accept the autonomy of those to whom they have given life, and this is never a painfree process. In Mary, it is vital that this process take place, so that she can become yet more empty of herself, yet more open to the working of the Holy Spirit within her, preparing her for the third redefinition of her motherhood. This is the sacrifice she must make on Golgotha *and* the gift she will receive there.

When she stands under the Cross, she is no longer referred to by her name. She is there only as "the mother of Jesus" (Jn 19:25). For now she must make the sacrifice of this motherhood: she must accept, not only that he is taken from her by death – a sacrifice great enough in itself, one might think – but that he first gives her to another as mother. To accept the will of the Father in the form of her child's death is itself a dying. But she must go even further: precisely at this moment, when all her human emotion is naturally concentrated on Jesus, she must begin to concern herself with "the disciple whom he loved". And once again, there is no personal name here. He stands there, not primarily as a specific historical individual, but as the representative of all the disciples whom Jesus loved and loves. She must expropriate herself of all the perfectly natural and laudable reactions of a mother, and take on a new maternal charge which is to know no limits.

It is sometimes said that Mary "receives John in exchange for Jesus"; this is a theme found in mediaeval sermons, where an elaborate rhetoric contrasts the two sons in order to underline the suffering of Our Lady under the Cross and make the hearers feel sorry for her. There is a vivid example of this rhetoric in a sermon of St Bernard (+ 1153) which is read in the Divine Office on the feast of Our Lady of Sorrows: "What an exchange! John was given to you in place of Jesus, a disciple in place of the Master, a son of Zebedee in place of the Son of God, a mere man in place of the true God. These words must have pierced your loving soul, since just to recall them breaks our hearts, hard and stony though they be." .

But this (with all respect for the mediaeval preachers) is not the central point here. Mary does not cease to be the mother of Jesus! Rather, her motherhood is widened to embrace all of us in the person of the beloved disciple. And he is told, "Behold, your mother." Part of Christian discipleship is what Pope John Paul II calls the "Marian dimension". This is a gift made by Jesus himself to all his disciples, and this means (as the Pope writes in his 1987 encyclical, *Redemptoris Mater*) that all Christians can find in Mary a path towards unity. Such a thought is highly startling to Catholics of my generation, who were given the impression as we grew up that non-Catholics had no relationship to Mary at all ("And Christian hateth Mary whom God kissed in Galilee", as G.K. Chesterton put it in his poem "Lepanto", set in the Reformation period); later, when ecumenical ideas began to spread, we were often given the related impression that Our Lady was a definite obstacle to ecumenism, and that it was far better to keep quiet about her. But the logic of the Pope's reflection is unassailable. If Jesus says to me and to all who follow him, "Behold, your mother", then we shall draw together, both within the Church and between the Churches, in looking together to Mary and learning from her motherly example.

We learn from Mary, as she stands under the Cross and accepts this extraordinary double expropriation of herself, that if we too accept that no limits may be set to what God has the "right" to demand of us, then in our lives too a totally unexpected horizon of service can open up.

We see this new horizon already in the Acts of the Apostles, where the apostles pray "with Mary the mother of Jesus" as they wait for the coming of the Holy Spirit (1:14). This is the last time that she is mentioned in the New Testament (although the "woman clothed with the sun" of Rev 12:1ff, a symbol of the messianic people, is intentionally reminiscent of Mary). But that does not mean that she disappears out of the Church's history; quite the contrary is true. If we relate the history of the Church, we are relating the history of Mary's maternal working, for she has (so to speak) disappeared *into* the mystery of the Church in such a way that the Body of Christ will always have a "Marian dimension".

This can be more or less visible; specific forms of devotion to Our Lady took time to develop. But whether or not believers have been conscious of her presence, she has always been active as a mother. She did not "become" Mother of the Church when Paul VI gave her this title in 1964. The title simply made explicit a reality that is as old as the Church herself. And the "price" of this motherly activity is the silent "yes" that Mary offers to the Father as she stands under the Cross of Jesus. This "yes", which transcends anything that she can understand intellectually at this point, and goes beyond the "rights" that could be claimed for her motherly emotions, is the "trigger" that lets loose in the Church this new motherhood – this new vocation – for the benefit of all Jesus' disciples.

What can this mean for us?

* * *

Our work is one of the principal factors of our identity. To be out of work is a deeply disorienting experience, especially if there is no realistic hope of finding employment, for this means that the challenges, the goals, the material rewards in terms of money and security, and the possibility of success (with the attendant esteem) are lacking in one's life. To lose one's work, particularly if one is at an age where it is improbable that one will find a new job, is perhaps even more disorienting in terms of one's identity and of relationships with other people; it can lead to the breakdown of marriage, where the partners have built up a network of expectation and self-definition that cannot adjust to the changed situation. These personal factors – quite apart from the economic issues involved – make the creation of jobs an urgent priority in modern societies.

These problems do not belong to some secular world far removed from the life of the Church of Christ. The Church is made up of human beings with basic human needs such as job-satisfaction, and basic human tendencies to define themselves, and let others define them, with reference to the work they carry out. Under-occupation and unemployment can pose genuine problems for priests and religious. Let me mention only three examples. (a) This can be the effect of demographic factors; I know some parishes where all the young people move away to find work, with the objective result that the only baptisms are of children whose parents return for the ceremony from the cities where they now live. (b) This can be one side-effect of the lack of vocations in recent years, which have forced many congregations to give up apostolates to which they had devoted themselves for many years. I recall one Mother General who told me that she had closed down fifty-two houses! In secular language, the problem is what to do with the local superiors who are now out of a job. Their field of responsibility has been taken from them, and they cannot all be given new posts of equivalent responsibility. (c) Or again, advancing years and ill health may make it necessary that one give up a work to which one has dedicated all one's energies.

The figure of Mary under the Cross is the figure of a woman who is required to give up one form of ministry. She is no longer required to exercise her motherly care for Jesus in the ways that a mother can show her concern and help a son, for the risen Jesus will not need that kind of service. He points her to a new ministry, one that is invisible to the eyes of the world but centrally important to the eyes of Christian faith. And this second ministry is much vaster in scope than the first. The first was historically limited to the early years of Jesus' life, in particular places, and it ceased on Golgotha. The new ministry as "Mother of the Church" knows no limits of time and space, and does not cease.

This too can become "my history". When one concrete possibility of serving the Lord is taken from me, even one in which I have invested very much of myself, I do not need to wither away altogether and consider myself useless. I mentioned in an earlier chapter the woman who discovered a new ministry at the age of ninety-three. In human terms, a sick or elderly person has little to contribute, and a parish priest of five hundred people does "less" than the parish priest of five thousand. But such worldly criteria have no real place in the Christian evaluation of ministry. Only God knows what is truly "efficient" (if we want to use such a word) in building up his kingdom.

If I find that it becomes harder and harder to do the *amount* of work (or of prayer) that I used to manage, this certainly does not automatically mean that my life is in fact less fruitful for the kingdom. We may think here of Thérèse of Lisieux dragging herself along the corridor of her Carmel and offering up each footstep for missionaries. Objectively, what was the contribution of this mortally sick young nun to the Church's missionary work? Nothing at all, in the eyes of the world, which sees only the externals – and literally boundless, in the eyes of God who sees the total picture.

We can sum up: as in the case of Mary, my second ministry, after I have had to give up my first, may be much vaster in scope than anything that went before it.

* * *

For this to happen, my faith must grow deeper and my renunciation must be based on a profound faith in the God who has called me and who is faithful to his promise to me, as he was faithful to Abram and all the others he called.

The renunciation which Mary makes under the Cross, transcending her own emotional responses to take on the new motherhood of Jesus' beloved disciple, is based on such a faith. This can be learned by us too.

An excellent piece of advice for those in a crisis is that they should widen their prayer out beyond themselves. Crises are normal in human life, especially when people live and work close together, perhaps especially in families and in religious communities. It is an obvious Christian reaction to pray for oneself, to pray for patience and strength. But we should pray for the others involved too. We should try to see them as Christ sees them, and include them in our intercession. This has a double effect. It makes God's help available for them, and it makes God's help available for ourselves; we have opened a space in the world through our intercession, a space in which he can act to transform a difficult situation.

But this principle has wider validity still. Those suffering from depression, exhaustion, illness, those searching for their path in life, those in crises of faith and hope, those in problems of any kind, can be recommended to pray for others. This act of transcending my own emotions, this act whereby I say to God that, no matter how terribly things may be going for me at the moment, I am not the whole of my concern and I do realise that other people need his help too, opens up springs of grace for them *and for myself.* This is something that I have experienced countless times in my own life and that I have recommended to many other people. It is extraordinarily efficacious in training us in the spirit of self-forgetfulness that will sustain us if we are called to the dying involved in giving up the work in which we have spent our life.

SISTERS OF NOTRE DAME
21 WELD ROAD
BIRKDALE, SOUTHPORT
1 PR8 2AZ

XI

Joseph's vocation

Joseph's vocation to be the foster father of Jesus is obviously not so central in salvation history as Mary's vocation to be his mother. But here too we can learn important lessons for our own calling to serve God. Here too, salvation history can become "my history".

The first important lesson for us lies in the very smallness of the things required of Joseph: "Do not fear to take Mary as your wife... she shall bear a son and you shall call his name Jesus" (Mt 1:20f). The actions involved here are small in themselves. They are not to be played out upon the great stage of public attention, like a royal wedding then or now. But they are essential in God's plan: Mary must be protected from any accusation of sexual misconduct, and Jesus must be acknowledged by Joseph as his own son – this is the legal significance of his giving the child a name – in order to protect him from any smear of illegitimacy. Joseph's role is small, but he cannot be deleted from the story of the birth of Christ.

The next three commands to Joseph ensure that the newborn Jesus will not fall victim to the attempts of the local rulers in Palestine to secure their throne against a potential rival. Matthew tells how the wise men from the east alarm Herod greatly with their question: "Where is the newborn king of the Jews? For we have seen his star in the east, and we have come to prostrate ourselves before him" (2:2). Herod is "struck all of a heap", says Matthew, and orders the massacre of all the male babies in Bethlehem as a precautionary measure. Doubt is often cast on the historical accuracy of these stories, sometimes for literary reasons, but sometimes also with recourse to arguments that assume that a king at that period would have behaved like one of ourselves: we do not believe in astrology and we find the politically motivated murder of infants repulsive, and "therefore" Herod cannot have done what Matthew says. But Herod was neither the first nor the last ruler to believe in astrology; for example, it was striking to see how few people rejected as implausible the allegations that Ronald Reagan regularly consulted an astrologer while he was President of the United States in the 1980's. And children have been massacred in cold blood, sometimes as an element in genocide (e.g. under Nazism or in Rwanda in 1994), but sometimes as a deliberate political act (e.g. by the Emperor Bokassa in what is now once more the Central African Republic, just before he was overthrown). There is (sadly enough) no reason to doubt the reality of the threat to Jesus' life. And it was vital that he should not fall into Herod's hands: for the death that would redeem us was not the murder of a helpless small child, but the free act of an adult's gift of himself. Once again, Joseph must protect the child and his mother, in order that God's plan can be carried out in the proper way.

It is here that Joseph receives God's directives: "Rise and take the child and his mother, and flee to Egypt, and remain there until I tell you: for Herod is about to search for the child in order to kill him" (2:13); "after the death of Herod, behold an angel of the Lord appeared in a dream to Joseph in Egypt and said, 'Rise and take the child and his mother and go to Israel'" (2:19f); "he was given instructions in a dream, and he went to the region of Galilee" (2:22). What he does is small in itself, but once again, we cannot delete him from the story. His service is an essential part of the whole narrative.

* *.*

We see the same kind of vocation in the New Testament's other Joseph, the Cypriot Levite whom the apostles call "Barnabas". Barnabas has various services to render as an apostle, but the most important thing he does in the Acts of the Apostles is to *further the vocation of someone else* – just like Joseph the husband of Mary. St Luke tells us that when the new convert Saul left Damascus and came to Jerusalem, "he attempted to join the disciples: and all were afraid of him, because they did not believe that he was a disciple" (9:26). Their fear seemed perfectly justified, humanly speaking. Only a short while before, Saul had been a violent persecutor of the disciples of Jesus in Jerusalem, one who "approved" of the killing of Stephen (8:1) and had gone to the trouble of getting some kind of official permit from the high priest to hunt down Christians in the synagogues at Damascus. His story about his conversion must have seemed improbable to them. In fact, they are bound to have believed him to be a spy or an *agent provocateur.*

Such figures are recurrent in Church history. They feature prominently in the history of Elizabethan Catholicism four hundred years ago, for example, or in the situation under communism in eastern Europe in our own century. I myself have a friend who was approached by the secret police while a seminarian in Romania. They told him that if he refused to act an informer on his fellow students, he would be expelled. He was to return in three days and tell them his decision. When he declined to collaborate, pressure was immediately put on the rector and the bishop – and he was expelled. The result of such situations is that "you never know who you are talking to", and this was the fear of the Church in Jerusalem.

Had they shut the doors permanently in the face of Saul, the whole history of Christianity would have been utterly different. The Church as a whole would have lost the man who understood the religious significance of Jesus more deeply and clearly than anyone else in the first century. At this crossroads, it is Barnabas who acts: "he took him by the hand and led him to the apostles, and explained to them how Saul had seen the Lord on the way and what he had said to him, and how Saul had spoken out boldly at Damascus in the name of Jesus" (9:27).

Paul's ministry in the Church at Jerusalem is very brief, because his disputes with the Hellenists so enrage them that they try to kill him. At this point, the "brothers" of the Church send Paul off to Tarsus. They still do not truly believe in him – what they want is peace for themselves, rather than the challenge of Paul's preaching, and there is surely a note of irony in Luke's use of the word "brothers" here (9:30). This is confirmed by the little Greek word *oun* in verse 31, to which Cardinal Carlo Maria Martini of Milan has drawn attention: "The brothers brought him down to Caesarea and sent him off to Tarsus. *Therefore* the Church throughout the whole of Judea and Galilee and Samaria had peace!" Most translations fail to pick up the bitterness in Luke's choice of words here, and either leave the word "therefore" out or weaken it ("and so...").

But this is an important point. The enforced inactivity of Saul in Tarsus would thwart God's plan for the growth of the Church, and once again it is Barnabas who takes action to bring Saul back to the ministry. When the Church in Jerusalem sends Barnabas to Antioch, "he left for Tarsus to look for Saul, and when he found him he brought him to Antioch. And they remained for a whole year in the Church and taught a great multitude, and it was in Antioch that the disciples were called Christians for the first time" (11:25f). We may presume that it was the distinctiveness of Paul's preaching that led to the new name.

The vocation of Joseph the husband of Mary is wholly at the service of her vocation and of the future "vocation" of the child Jesus. The vocation of Joseph Barnabas is to open the doors which a merely human reaction and reasoning have closed to the vocation of Paul. Neither Joseph is a central figure, and what they do is modest, if taken by itself. But if they had said "no" to God's call to them, letting themselves be guided by human criteria rather than by faith, Mary would have had no husband, and Paul would have languished idle in Tarsus. Human thinking would have concluded that Mary's child was conceived in infidelity, and that Paul was a dangerous troublemaker who was too much for the Church to handle. Their "small steps" (to borrow the famous words spoken in 1969 on the Moon) are a "giant leap" for the Church in the history of salvation.

* * *

The lesson for us is straightforward. God does call a few disciples to carry out exceptional ministries. But we cannot all be Mother General or Cardinal Archbishop (or at least, not all at the same time), and many disciples are given the vocation of helping these others to perform their exceptional ministries. A particular form of this calling can be the ministry of teacher. I imagine that almost all who teach will have had my experience of teaching students who have greater gifts than I myself have: I am Barnabas to their Paul. As I observed in an earlier chapter, one can be called to minister spiritually to people who are far in advance of oneself – you do not have to be a saint yourself before you can hear the confession of someone who is a saint! And in a more general sense, all kinds of auxiliary activities (typing letters for someone else, taking people in a car to the airport, setting out the chairs in a room where someone else is going to give a talk) are my collaboration in what God does through the ministry of others. Like Joseph, I am an essential part of the story precisely in (and not despite) the smallness of the service God calls me to render.

To speak of "centrality" or "exceptional ministries" does not imply that one service is more *important* than another. The Pope is not more important than Peppina, nor Peppina more important than the Pope! But it is true that some ministries make their specific and invaluable contribution to the kingdom of God by being *ordered to* other ministries.

* * *

We can develop this insight by means of a second reflection on St Joseph's vocation. Apart from the infancy narratives of Matthew and Luke, he never appears in the Gospels, and it is generally assumed that he has died before Jesus' public ministry begins. This means that he dies without seeing the "point" or the "fruit" of what God had called him to do for the child Jesus and Mary his mother. When he dies, Jesus is presumably still working as a young carpenter in Nazareth.

We too may die without seeing the point or the fruit of what God has called us to do, especially if that was something without great external drama. This experience too can be illuminated by the figure of Joseph in Nazareth, when we consider the sheer *monotony* of his life as a carpenter who would have had much the same kind of work to do week after week, without the natural rhythms and changes of the farmer or fisherman. Add to this the dullness of life in a proverbially dull village ("Can anything good come out of Nazareth?" asks Nathanael cynically, Jn 1:46), with none of the mass media that link life in a village today with life in the rest of the world. The temptation to lose sight of the longer-term plans of God, to sink down into the humdrum details of every day, to envy those who lead a supposedly "richer" and more "fulfilling" life in material terms, or those who are serving God in a more public and thus supposedly more "important" way, is very great. To live day by day for God, "preparing the way of the Lord" in a completely undramatic life, demands a profound faith and faithfulness.

This reflection links up with what I wrote in chapter VI about "hanging on" in situations of suffering and the temptation to give up. Here, where the problem is the monotony of one's ministry, the same principle applies: we must hang on, trusting in faith that our work too prepares the way of the Lord just as St Joseph's work in the carpenter's shop prepared the way for Jesus, ensuring that the Holy Family had enough to eat. That may sound prosaic, when compared to the ministry of John the Baptist, but take away Joseph and there would have been no Jesus for John the Baptist to proclaim. The prosaic work is essential.

When the liturgical feast of the Holy Family is celebrated after Christmas, we tend to talk about the quality of relationships within families; the religious families (like those inspired by Charles de Foucauld, + 1916) that look to Nazareth as the centre of their spirituality tend to aim at a particular quality of contemplative silence. All of this doubtless reflects qualities of love and silence that were actually present in Nazareth. But there is a danger that we may overlook the dullness of their life, day in and day out doing the same kind of work, thereby underestimating the fidelity of Mary and Joseph to their vocations in the "hidden" years of Jesus' life.

One of the oddest books on my shelves has the virtue of emphasising the monotony of life at Nazareth. It is a collection of private revelations allegedly communicated by Our Lady to a woman in Italy in the early 1980's and published under the title "My life at Nazareth" (*La mia vita a Nazareth*). I have never met the seer, and I would not care to argue for the authenticity of what is written in her book, which has a stupefying banality about it: "Father Joseph, can I have some more olives?" says Jesus at one point, and Joseph replies, "Of course, all you have to do is to ask, but you must always ask, because that is what good boys do." The vegetables Mary cooks are described in minute detail, as are the flowers in the garden, and Jesus asks his heavenly Father in his night prayers to give all the children toasted bread with honey... I repeat that I break no lances for the authenticity of these "revelations". And yet life at Nazareth must have been pretty much like that. The gospels are silent for the simple reason that there was *nothing to say* about those years. But these are the years that laid the foundation of the public ministry and the passion of

Jesus. These are the years in which he became an adult. And these are the years in which Joseph lives his vocation as Jesus' foster father.

No angels fly to and fro, no miracles are performed by Jesus, no parables are spoken. Everything is perfectly ordinary, as far as the people of the village can see – so ordinary that the Gospels tell us the townspeople of Nazareth could not accept the public ministry of Jesus: "Is not this the carpenter?" (Mk 6:3). They know him, and whatever other villages may do, *they* are not going to be taken in by him! Jesus has to leave and set up his headquarters at Capharnaum. And yet the ordinariness of the life of the Holy Family, far from discrediting Jesus in our eyes – the eyes of faith in him – is a sign of the genuineness of the incarnation, and of the greatness of Mary and Joseph as they respond to their vocations in salvation history.

This is what life is like for the overwhelming majority of those whom the Lord calls. We prepare the way of the Lord in an undramatic service that is often hidden even from those who benefit most directly from it. But if we reflect on the figure of St Joseph at Nazareth, we can see that no service is ever too small or hidden, no form of life is ever too monotonous: for if in all we do, we keep in mind that it is the Lord whom we are serving, then we can have the faith to say that our work too is an indispensable part of his work in building up his kingdom. Humanly speaking, I may be nothing more than a footnote in a doctoral thesis that someone will write a hundred years from now – if indeed I am as much as that! But for the God whom I serve, there are no "footnotes", and "your Father, who sees what is done in secret, will give you your reward" (Mt 6:6). The reward of Joseph can be ours, if we open our eyes in faith to see the dignity of our apparently modest vocation.

XII

Not servants but friends

In the chapter about the Visitation, I wrote that Mary and Paul are proud to call themselves "slaves" and that this is a word which, understood in all its radicality, expresses something essential to every vocation. This, however, needs to be complemented in this chapter by a reflection on the words of Jesus to his disciples before his passion, "No longer do I call you slaves, because the slave does not know what his lord is doing: no, I have called you friends, because I have made known to you all that I have heard from my Father" (Jn 15:15). These words do not cancel out the truth of what has been said above about our role as "slaves". This remains the truth, as seen from our perspective. Seen from the perspective of the Lord who has called us, however, we are not servants but friends.

The first chapter of John contains a significant narrative of the call of two disciples. John the Baptist points out Jesus to two of his own disciples with the words, "Behold the Lamb of God" (1:36). On hearing this, they set out after Jesus, who "turned round and, seeing them follow him, said to them, 'What are you looking for?' They said to him, 'Rabbi' (which means 'Teacher' in translation), 'where are you staying?' He said to them, 'Come, and you will see.'" The two disciples of John the Baptist begin by "following" Jesus in the literal sense that they are walking behind him; this is transformed through their dialogue with him into a "following" in the religious sense. His question implies that something deep is at stake: it is a challenge to them to say what they are *really* looking for. Their reply, with its title "Rabbi", gives the answer. They are looking for a rabbi who can teach them. A rabbi then was not like a professor of theology today, who teaches by giving lectures and writing books, one with whom the individual students may well have no personal contact at all. One learned from a rabbi by living with him, sharing his meals, watching how he reacted to the various situations and problems, seeing how his teaching was embedded in his relationship to God, noting the quality of his family life. Theology was not something to be taught neutrally in a classroom, but something to be transmitted through the whole of the life that the student was permitted to share. This is what the disciples have in mind when they ask, "Rabbi, where are you staying?" They want to come and live under Jesus' roof, sharing his meals and absorbing his teaching day by day through watching him and noting *how he lives.*

Jesus did not in fact "stay" in one place. He moved about and affirmed that he had "nowhere to lay his head" (Lk 9:58). But wherever he went, the disciples accompanied him, watching and listening and absorbing the teaching that his whole life imparted. Jesus held no lectures and wrote no books. But he taught all the same: "He was praying in a certain place, and when he had finished, one of his disciples said to him, 'Lord, teach us to pray, as John too taught his disciples'" (Lk 11:1). The response of Jesus is not a theoretical instruction, but a prayer – the Lucan version of the Lord's Prayer. It is by doing what Jesus does, by addressing God as "Father" just like Jesus, that the disciples will learn from him.

The life of those whom Jesus calls to follow him – in the Gospels and today – means that they become his friends. They share his table, they live under the same roof with him (when he has a roof to offer), they go with him along the streets of Galilee, seeing how he reacts to people and situations, noting what his priorities are, how he uses his time, the place that prayer has for him. He calls them to depart, like Abram, from what is familiar and to set out *with himself* as teacher and companion. Their new "home", the place where they belong and where they can truly be themselves, is their friendship with Jesus. This means that for us, as for the disciples who followed him in Palestine, Jesus must be the centre of our lives. And this means: not as an idea, still less an ideology, but as a living person: "although you did not see him with your own eyes" (unlike the disciples in the Gospel story), "you love him; and although you still do not see him, you believe in him and rejoice with an unutterable and glorious joy" (1 Pet 1:8). This is what is meant by a phrase I have often heard Evangelical Christians in England use: "Jesus our contemporary". He is not held fast in history like a butterfly pinned by a collector to his showcase. Every generation can say to him, "Rabbi, where are you staying?", and hear his reply, "Come, and you will see." While he was on earth, he was limited to one particular place and time, but now that he is in heaven, he has become accessible to all generations in all places, and he can speak directly to any of us today, just as he did then, and invite us to share his life as his friends.

* * *

This fellowship with Jesus is always, and necessarily, fellowship with the other disciples who follow him. To put this point theologically: to say "yes" to Jesus is always implicitly to say "yes" to his Church. When Blessed Edith Stein came to faith in Jesus in the summer of 1921, the logic of this encounter with him was the baptism she received a few months later, thereby entering the Church. Jesus is at work outside the visible community of the Church, for he is, objectively speaking, Lord of all humanity, whether or not all humanity acknowledges his lordship. But membership of the visible community is not an optional extra for those who come to recognise him as the living Saviour who speaks to them personally, for it is only within this visible community that they can find the normal sacramental relationship to Jesus their contemporary.

But one does not enter the Church because of the other disciples. The basis of the fellowship Christians have with one another is Christ's call to each individual disciple, whether this is a call to enter the Church from outside, or a call to one already baptised to *live* what baptism means. The fellowship with the others is the outcome of this individual fellowship with Jesus, and is a gift that thus transcends merely human sympathy and friendship. This is something we see in the group of the Twelve. Each is called as an individual by Jesus, but this call makes them members of a community: "he called to him those he wished, and they came to him. And he appointed twelve, whom he also called apostles, so that they might be with him, and so that he might send them out..." (Mk 3:13f). The lists of the Twelve do not agree entirely about their names, and it is clear that not all of them were equally important as individuals in the history of the first decades of the Church. But if we take the list which Luke gives, and read it in the light of what Matthew tells us, we have a very interesting clue to what Jesus intends the Church "built on the foundation of the apostles" (Eph 2:20) to be.

Jesus chose "those he wished", says Mark, and Luke's list (6:14ff) begins with two pairs of brothers, "Simon, whom he called Peter, and Andrew his brother, and James and John". Here, Jesus seems to be building on the human sympathy born of family ties. The list continues with Philip, their friend from Bethsaida (cf. Jn 1:44) – here, human friendship is the base on which Jesus builds his community. But two later names cannot be accounted for on the basis of human sympathies: "Matthew... and Simon who was called the Zealot". The two names are not placed side by side, but twelve is after all not an enormous number, and Matthew and Simon must have seen each other at close quarters every day in Jesus' company. To understand the strangeness of Jesus' initiative in calling these two men to

128

be part of one group, we must recall the political/religious situation in which he began his ministry.

The Roman occupation of Palestine was not simply a political issue. It raised a specifically theological question which we see often in the Old Testament too: if God is still faithful to his people, why does he allow this to happen? If he is punishing us for our sins, what should his people do in order to win back his favour? The answer given by the groups called Zealots looked back to the stories of God's military deliverance of Israel, and they offered themselves to him as his military instruments to be used in driving out the Romans. It would therefore be wrong to dismiss them as terrorists, since they were inspired by theological motives, above all by their conviction that God is a God who acts in history to show his love for his people. They were particularly active in Galilee. When Luke says that the second Simon among the Twelve was "called the Zealot", this is to be understood in the full ideological sense of the word. This Simon was convinced of the theological justification of violence against the Romans.

Matthew's background is completely different. The tax-collector Levi whom Jesus calls to follow him (cf. Mk 2:13ff, Lk 5:27) is called Matthew in the Gospel which we call "Matthew's Gospel" (9:9ff). Tax-collectors have never been popular, but there was a particular reason for a Zealot like Simon to hate collaborators with the Romans, men who bid for a contract to raise taxes and extorted as much as they could from their fellow Jews. Anyone who collaborated with the Romans was a sinner against God in a Zealot's eyes. Even Jesus himself is recorded as coupling "Gentiles and tax-collectors" (cf. Mt 18:17, and 5:46f) as people who do not belong inside the community of the kingdom of God – the Gentiles for the obvious reason that they are by definition non-Jews, the tax-collectors because they have excluded themselves from Israel by their collaboration with the occupying power. The proper *religious* response of a Zealot to a tax-collector would presumably have been to kill him. (The idea of killing as an act of worship is not limited to Ayatollah Khomenei's *fatwa* against the novelist Salman Rushdie; Jesus himself warns his disciples, "The time will come when everyone who kills you will think he is offering worship to God", Jn 16:2.) As for Matthew, a tax-collector outside the fold, we cannot imagine that he would want to seek out the company of the Zealot Simon, who would want to kill him!

Jesus brings together within the Twelve these two men who could have nothing whatsoever in common, humanly and religiously speaking. This underlines the vitally important message that the only basis for their fellowship is *the person of Jesus himself.*

The twelve apostles are chosen to be the foundation of the new Israel, just as the twelve sons of Jacob were the foundation of the Israel in the old covenant. The distinction is clear: the old covenant is built on twelve brothers, while the new is built on a group that transcends the ties of blood or merely human friendship, a group that includes within itself men who would otherwise have been bitter enemies. And despite their disputes about which of them was the greatest, they remain basically united, because the "cement" that holds them together is the person of Jesus Christ. He loves each of them with an equal love and has called all of them together "so that they might be with him, and so that he might send them out". The paths along which they come to him are various. Two are led to Jesus by John the Baptist, Andrew fetches his brother Simon, Jesus "passes by" and calls them. But the end result is the same, an equality in love, a fellowship that looks continuously and exclusively to Jesus for its raison d'être.

* * *

Jesus has not lost his power to reconcile persons who are humanly irreconcilable. I experienced this myself in spring 1982, when we had an Argentinian seminarian as a guest in our monastery outside Rome. Shortly after he arrived, Argentina invaded the Falkland Islands, and we found ourselves sincerely divided, with him hoping that the Argentinians would keep what he called the Malvinas, and myself hoping that the British would reconquer what I called the Falklands. The end result, as one can see with hindsight, can be considered positive for both countries, since the loss of the islands was a "trigger" that overturned the military dictatorship in Buenos Aires. But at the time, it was not at all clear how things would turn out, and we watched the television news together each evening with no idea of how things would go. Each of us had his own ideas about that; I must admit that I was surprised to find in myself sentiments that I did not much like, a patriotism that seemed to tend towards unhealthy chauvinism. The same was true of him. But this division of convictions never affected life in the community; by common consent, we avoided talking about the war in the South Atlantic, and the only crisis came when the Bishop arrived for lunch one day. When he was introduced to the Argentinian, he pointed a finger of rebuke at him with the words, "Those islands are English!" The Abbot gasped and deftly changed the subject...

The awareness of fundamental unity in Jesus Christ the common Lord transcended our political discord. He united Matthew and Simon in the community of the Twelve, and he united us in prayer and daily living in the monastery in 1982.

He can also bring unity to those who seem to themselves and to others to have taken up incompatible religious positions. I remember a priest telling me in the mid-1970's about a community he knew: "I admire those Sisters," he said. "Half of them think it is a mortal sin not to wear the habit, and half of them think it is a mortal sin to wear the habit. But they hold together as a community!" This was a question both groups of Sisters saw as essential to the question of their communal identity, and such matters are obviously much more difficult than the response one makes to events completely outside the walls of the monastery, like a war thousands of miles away. The response of human logic to such situations is either for individuals who are "different" (and therefore potential troublemakers) to be pushed out, or else for them to give up in despair and leave. In some cases, there has been a split into two separate new communities, or even into separate new congregations, because the daily tensions arising from the irreconcilable religious positions are experienced as insupportable. The practical problems may appear insurmountable: how does a community or a congregation react when some of its members want to take on a new form of apostolate which they judge to be more in keeping with the charism of the founders? How does one hold widely diverging spiritualities within one and the same community? What if the religious positions harden into theological and/ or political stances (or "options")?

Anyone familiar with what has happened in the Church, and more specifically within religious life, since the Second Vatican Council, can put concrete names and faces and supply geographical and historical detail to everything written in the last paragraph. There may perhaps be no straightforward answer to such questions. But having asked them, I ought at least to indicate where an answer can be found.

I shall begin with an example drawn from a remote crisis, the so-called "paschal controversy" of the second century caused by the fact that Easter was celebrated on different dates in east and west. This was perceived on both sides as an essential matter of the Church's life. In the 150's, Polycarp of Smyrna visited Anicetus of Rome to discuss this controversy. Both sides appealed to apostolic traditions, and neither could persuade the other. They agreed to differ within the unity of the Church, as St Polycarp's disciple Irenaeus relates: "they maintained communion with one another, and in the church Anicetus yielded the eucharist to Polycarp, clearly because of respect. So they parted from one another in peace, and the whole Church was at peace, both those who observed the custom and those who did not". The expression "yielded the eucharist" means that the Pope invited the Asian bishop to preside at the celebration of the liturgy: there could be no clearer sign that they perceived their common oneness in Jesus Christ to be deeper than their division. They have a good claim to be venerated as the patron saints of a genuine ecumenism (inside the Church and also between the Churches) which does not gloss over serious problems, but which is nevertheless resolved to hold on firmly to the gift of unity in the person of Jesus.

The same crisis flared up many times later, precisely because it was regarded as such a central question, but the course of history has brought us to the end of the twentieth century, where within the unity of the one Catholic Church Easter is not in fact celebrated by everyone on the same date. Most follow the Gregorian Calendar, but there are some who still follow the Julian Calendar, such as the Byzantine Catholics in the Ukraine; and Catholic minorities in countries where most of the Christians belong to one or other Orthodox Church, such as Iraq, while otherwise observing the Gregorian Calendar, "go Julian" for the Easter cycle so that all the Christians in the country can unite in celebrating the liturgical feasts of our common redemption on the same date. No one perceives this as a deadly threat to the unity of the Church.

This does not mean that we understand the meaning of the Gospel "better" than Anicetus and Polycarp, who were somehow "wrong" to attach so much importance to the date of Easter. They lived and served Christ as disciples in their own particular period with its theological understanding and spiritual insight, and it was there that they took the decision to preserve communion. It is much easier to destroy unity in the name of a clear-cut theological logic which sees the alternatives as mutually exclusive. This is what Victor I of Rome did in the 190's when he excommunicated those Asian Churches which celebrated Easter on a different day from himself, provoking St Irenaeus to write the letter which tells us about Polycarp's visit to Rome forty years earlier. It is hard to live with spiritual untidiness, leaving it to the Holy Spirit to inspire a resolution of our discord in some future higher synthesis! Our task as members of the one Church of Jesus Christ is to hang on, without giving in to the temptations of a premature synthesis that would kill both the tensions and the life that generated them.

* * *

No one lives outside of time, and this means that this book is not being written in ignorance of the public conflicts in the Catholic Church today. Nor is it unrelated to them, as if spirituality could be written in abstraction from the concrete context of the living fellowship of the Church and from the theological and other questions that matter to believers. This in turn means that I must specify as far as possible *how* what I am writing is related to these conflicts. Let me take a concrete example.

On 13 January 1995, Jacques Gaillot was deposed by the Vatican as Bishop of Evreux in France. The reason given in the official communiqué was that he had "unfortunately shown himself unsuited to exercise the office of unity, which is the first task of a bishop". This virtually unparalleled act unleashed a storm of reactions, many focussing on the personality and/or specific acts of this one bishop, or of Pope John Paul II. But other, deeper reactions revealed *conflicting* understandings of *theological questions* which the disputants *agreed* were essential to the life of the Church. Fundamental questions were asked about the role of an individual bishop inside his diocese and outside it, about the role of an episcopal conference, about the role of the Vatican in the life of the Church, and here there was agreement that such matters were vital to all Catholics.

The detailed discussion such theological questions deserve takes us outside the specific purpose of this book. I would only emphasise that the example of Anicetus and Polycarp should make us pause and reflect very carefully, before we assert that the divergent positions on the theological issues today are so irreconcilable that they destroy the essential unity in Jesus Christ. *Sentire cum ecclesia,* the attitude of allowing all that concerns the Church to concern myself too, means that I open myself to *all* the various kinds of suffering that exist within the fellowship of believers today: specifically, this means that whether I am sincerely pro-Gaillot or sincerely contra-Gaillot, I nevertheless try to accept *into my heart* the suffering of those who disagree with my own position, and resist the temptation to permit even sincere divergences on deep levels to polarise us and to tear the fabric of the Church's unity, which mediaeval writers so often compared to the seamless robe of Christ. This is a challenge to an authentically ecclesial spirituality, and it is immensely costly. It has nothing in common with a "spiritualisation" that flinches from facing up to conflicts!

* * *

If this is true on a global level – taking the tensions and disputes of the Church as a whole, or of one diocese or religious congregation as a whole, it can also be applicable to the smaller world of one particular parish, or one particular religious house. Often, when deeply-held convictions conflict and clash and wound, we do just have to hang on, and let time resolve the issues at stake. But it is not always possible in practice to adopt a strategy of waiting. What do we do in practice, when the gulf between conflicting ideas seems to be unbridgeable?

There are two distinct situations here.

135

(1) In the first situation, the issues in the debate are not in fact fundamental to those who are locked in conflict. I have seen this often – indeed, with a tiresome regularity – in my own community, when a clothing or a profession or an ordination was drawing near. It was precisely then, as these times of grace were approaching, that doors began to be slammed, voices raised, nasty comments made, and that theological and spiritual conflicts arose. The very regularity of these conflicts began to suggest to me that what was at issue was not really a theological question or a dissension in spirituality: these things were not significant in themselves, but were the symptoms of a much deeper conflict, the conflict between good and evil in the community as a whole, which was being offered God's grace *as a community* and was putting up the same kind of resistance *as a community* that one finds in oneself as an individual. And as I have said, this individual resistance to God's deep working usually manifests itself in sexual temptations and *feelings of aggression*. Once one has seen that, the surface conflicts in a monastery take on different dimensions. In one sense, one no longer takes them quite so seriously, because they are not the real problem. The real problem that has to be tackled by the community as a whole is the quality of their response to the gifts of God. They have to learn to look, as a community, below the surface squalls and to check whether they are still securely anchored in God as a community. If the anchor is secure, they will ride out the squalls; if not, the ship will break up. It is always essential to ask, "What is really going on here?" We must not stop short at the surface crises, as if they were the whole reality.

In any case, crises and tensions are part of human life, since we are all fallen. Religious life is no more difficult than family life! When things go badly, it can help to take the very simple step of looking at the other person(s) with whom we have problems, while they are receiving communion. What do we see? We see, coming towards them, the same absolute and unconditional love of Jesus Christ that comes towards ourselves when we receive communion. If the Lord has called this difficult person (this Simon the Zealot, perhaps) to serve him, prompted by exactly the same love with which he has called me (this Matthew) to serve him, making no distinctions in the intensity of his self-giving to that person and to me, then what right do I have to make distinctions?

It may be that I am convinced that the other person is not living the consecration to God which he or she has vowed to live. But here I must refrain from examining the conscience of others: "Who are you to judge the servant of *another*?" says Paul (Rom 14:4). At the last day, it is God who will sit on the judgment seat, and so I can safely commit judgment to him now. Besides this, I will find plenty to keep me occupied, if I examine my own conscience: and if I hope to find forgiveness from the Lord for my sins (which are perhaps less visible than those of others), must I not be willing to have the same hope for them? For once again, there are no gradations in the Lord's love for those he calls, and any distinctions or reservations that I would like to introduce are inevitably false.

The proper reaction to all such difficulties is to pray for those who cause them for us. In general, I have the impression that while religious communities are good at praying with each other, they tend very much to neglect the duty of praying *for* each other. Indeed, in crises – when this would be more important than ever – one can even stop praying for those for whom one had been praying previously. But those with whom we live are entrusted in a particular way to our intercession. It is through such intercession, especially for those who cause us problems, that we grow into the supernatural friendship that is meant to be characteristic of the disciples of Jesus.

Personal conflicts in marriage or the consecrated life often bring the temptation to resolve them by getting out. The cultural atmosphere which we breathe in every day does not encourage us to cope with tensions in human relationships by staying where we are! But these tensions ought rather to be the opportunity for a deeper reflection on why I am where I am. If it is the response to a call by the Lord, then human difficulties by themselves can never be a sufficient reason for me to give up.

One dangerous strategy for those who find community life or married life difficult is to look for emotional satisfaction outside. We direct our emotional energy outwards, for example to those whom we serve in teaching, or in the caring professions, where it is easier for us to show what fine people we are and to reap a harvest of gratitude, appreciation and affectionate praise, since those we serve do not see the negative sides of our personality – we reserve those for the unfortunate members of our community or our family. A great deal has been written about this by psychologists, and we ought to be aware of the spiritual dimension of this problem, which is more subtle (and hence in fact more dangerous) than any specifically sexual temptation, for we would recognise that much more easily as a "temptation", or as a "sin" if we yielded to it.

When we do yield here, we only increase the difficulties of the religious or family life we are leading. We must show love, not only to those whom we serve, but also to those with whom we share our lives. They, who assuredly will not have any illusions about us, have also the first claim upon us as persons called to love.

* * *

(2) In the second kind of conflict situation, those divided do perceive the matters involved as truly essential. Questions of spirituality, which ought to enrich a community through its individual members, can in fact divide it. If one member is perceived by the others as seeking and finding spiritual nourishment outside the prayer life of the community, this can easily disrupt unity. How do the

others react when this person says that participation in such forms of prayer is "essential" for him/her?

We can see the fundamental answer to this question if we pursue our reflections on the presence of both Matthew and Simon the Zealot in the community of the Twelve. Jesus' call to them to follow him does not leave them untouched in their deepest convictions: it is a call to conversion through which, by finding Jesus and saying "yes" to him, they likewise find each other and say "yes" to each other. The enmity – not merely human and political, but also a religious enmity – is transformed into a genuine fellowship in the Jesus whom *both of them* serve and love. In the same way, Jesus does not leave us untouched in our deepest convictions, but calls each one to a conversion. In order to say "yes" to him, we must let him *relativise* our own estimate of what is "essential". And we can find that this is very costly indeed. The price of unity within our communities is sometimes very high, for it can mean a mutual *compromise* in matters we regard as essential.

We tend to assume that compromise means defeat for one side, and this may be true in political and social life. But in the context of the Church's life, compromise should mean an authentic encounter that brings the two sides out of their mutual hostility and on to a common ground. This is what happens at the meeting between Paul and Peter at Jerusalem which is described in Gal 2:1ff. Paul and Peter have been divided by the activities of the "false brothers", so that the unity of the Church is in very grave danger. Is the mission to the Gentiles to be conducted on Paul's terms, or on James's terms? It looks like a straight "either/or", but a genuine compromise involving no defeat is reached, sealed by the "right hand of fellowship" given by Paul and the "pillars", James and Cephas and John: "we were to go to the Gentiles and they to the Jews". This division of labours could, of course, lead in turn to a *de facto* separation, and so Paul is charged "to remember the poor" among the Church in Jerusalem. By organising the collection of funds for their relief, he displays in a concrete way the love that holds *all* the disciples of Jesus together in the one communion. Thus the compromise entered into from both sides brings into existence a new reality, a deeper unity which finds expression in practical charity. No one is "defeated".

Are we willing to let this point of salvation history become "my history", the history of my community? We should never underestimate the difficulties: if we keep to our present example, we see from the New Testament and the whole of Church history how exceedingly hard it is to accept genuine compromise.

We see this from the next section of Galatians, in which Paul relates that James was not faithful to the accord they had reached, but sent emissaries to Antioch to undermine his preaching. In the second century, the tables were turned, and Gentile Christians succeeded in driving out of the Church those Jewish Christians who still wished to observe the Law of Moses. In our century, there are small groups of Jewish Christians in America and in Israel who seek to develop an authentically Jewish form of Christianity which would be faithful to both the Law of Moses and the new law of Jesus. If they succeed in this, we shall return to the hopeful and difficult perspectives of St Paul's ministry: "Although I am free from all, I have made myself the slave of all... I have become everything to everyone" (1 Cor 9:19ff). This is the ministry of one who brings peace where there is division.

A deep conversion is required, an uprooting from one's own habits and unexamined prejudices, to go out to meet the other person, the stranger who can become my brother or my sister in the one Lord who calls both of us to be, not servants but friends – friends with himself and friends with one another. Am I willing to die to myself in this way? Am I willing to set out like Abram? If not, the Church will never find unity in itself (to say nothing of ecumenical hopes). But if I am willing, like Matthew and Simon the

Zealot, or like Peter and Paul at their meeting in Jerusalem, to take the risks of compromise, the result can be "the right hand of fellowship" in a common service.

"For he is our peace, who has made the two one... so that he might create in himself one new person out of the two, making peace and reconciling them both in one body to God through the Cross, killing their enmity on it" (Eph 2:14ff). If he could reconcile Jew and Gentile through his Cross, creating a new unity "in himself", are we really going to maintain that our little divisions are insuperable? That would be merely a statement about our laziness and our intolerance, not in the least a statement about what he is able to do in us, if we open ourselves to the creative power of his crucified – and crucifying – love.

XIII

Peter: vocation and forgiveness

According to Luke's narrative of the specific calling of
St Peter (5:1-11), the decisive encounter with Jesus is above
all the encounter with holiness, a holiness that shows Peter
his own sinfulness and makes him cry out, "Depart from
me, for I am a sinful man, O Lord!" (5:8). Luke writes that
"terror had seized him".

This was not the first encounter in Luke's Gospel between Simon and Jesus. Jesus has already "gone into the
house of Simon" and cured his mother-in-law of a high
fever (4:38ff), and Simon has seen how Jesus cured all the
sick who were brought to him on that same evening. And
we see from his words to Jesus on the lake that he is
already a disciple, not merely an admirer of the worker of
miracles: when Jesus tells the fishermen to let down their
nets for a catch, Simon replies, "Teacher, we have toiled all
night without taking anything. But *at your word* I will let
down the nets" (5:5). These words are a profession of faith.
The experienced fisher knows perfectly well that the con-
ditions for a catch are unfavourable, but "at your word" he
lets down his nets. The result is a catch so heavy that the
boats begin to sink. This miracle is much more for Peter
than merely a dramatic wonder: it is the "trigger" of a
deeper faith, because it discloses to him both who Jesus is
and who he himself is. The contrast is too great, and so he
cries out, "Depart from me!"

But Jesus does not accept this reaction. He says to
Simon, "Do not be afraid! From now on, it is human beings
you will be catching." And Luke concludes: "And when
they had brought the boats to land, they left everything and
followed him."

The encounter with Jesus is always the encounter with his holiness and the disclosure of our unworthiness. Just as Peter tells him to go away, just as the centurion sends friends to tell him that he is not worthy to have Jesus come under his roof (Lk 7:6), so the one called today experiences a radical unworthiness that reacts defensively and wants to refuse the call for this reason. We have seen, especially in those called in the old covenant, that the incompetence of the one called is no barrier to God's working – indeed, the incompetence of the human minister shows all the more clearly that it is the omnipotent God who is at work, and so there will be no tendency to ascribe to oneself the victories achieved by the divine power. In the case of Peter, we see a further, deeper dimension of this same principle. Jesus does not call one who is sinless to be a fisher of men: he calls one who is deeply aware of his own sinfulness.

And as we see in the Gospels, this sinfulness is not merely a tendency to sin, a potential for being tempted to fall away from God. Peter is one who sins in a very dramatic way, by solemnly denying that he is a disciple of Jesus. Here too, we see that the apostolic activity of the one called can be ascribed only to the power of the holy God, and never to the sinful apostle. And this is very significant for our own vocations.

* * *

The realisation of my sinfulness – assuming that I do accept this fact, without trying to neutralise and "psychologise" my sin – ought to lead me, not to refuse the Lord's call to follow him, but to seek the encounter with his forgiveness in the sacrament of penance. For the most fundamental reality about myself is not that "I am a sinner" (a sentence with myself as the subject), but that "God calls me and loves me" (a sentence with him as the subject). The realisation of my sinfulness is meant to point me out beyond my own self, to the one who forgives.

It is never easy, psychologically speaking, to confess to another person that I have sinned. Even if I am fully aware that the priest too is a sinner, there is always an obstacle to be overcome before I can admit what I have done or failed to do. (If this were not the case, it would mean that I was proud of my sins!) But this psychological difficulty, the requirement that I die to myself in order to confess my sin, points to the deeper dimensions of the sacrament, which brings me down *into the death of Christ,* who died a sinner's death on the Cross. My little "dying" in the humility of confession unites me to his great dying on my behalf and *in my place.* And the priest's absolution gives me a share in the new life of Christ's resurrection. Just as the resurrection is the absolute gift of the Father to the Son, so forgiveness is the absolute gift of the Lord to the penitent. I have died to my sins and now he gives me a fresh start.

I remember once a priest looking at me with a rather worried expression, after I had confessed my sins. He then said, "You know, Father Brian, ideally we ought to come so far that we no longer need to go to confession!" This sounds logical enough: progress in the Christian life ought to mean that we no longer needed this sacrament, for the simple reason that we had stopped committing any sins. So I began to be rather worried too. But a very little reflection showed me that reality is diametrically opposite to what this priest had said. The closer we draw to God, the more profoundly do we become aware of how far we are from him, and the more deeply do we see our need of the sacrament of reconciliation.

Even if we find ourselves confessing the same sins over and over again for years on end, this is only a reminder that we remain the same person, with the same temptations and tendencies. This does not mean that confession and absolution are ineffective and that we should therefore give up the sacrament, but rather that the sacrament is like a leaven that works slowly in our lives to configure us to the life of Christ within us. And so we can try to learn patience with ourselves – just as God is patient with us! I may know perfectly well that I am going to commit again tomorrow the sins I am confessing today. But God knows this too, and he does not wash his hands of me. He knows that his grace is ultimately more powerful than my sinfulness, precisely because his Son has died for me and has set his seal upon me in baptism, and because on my side, I have said "yes" to him – it may as yet be a weak "yes", but it does give the Lord *something* to work on. Even if I have to struggle for sixty years with the same temptations and the same sins, I should never be less optimistic about myself than God. Sin is sin, and we should never play down its seriousness, but the last word belongs to the one who says, "I have conquered the world" (Jn 16:33).

Sacramental confession therefore remains a part – or better, a dimension – of the life of the one called by God to serve him. Because for us, as for Peter, the encounter with Jesus every day is an encounter with his holiness, we must enter into the paschal mystery of his death and resurrection through the sacrament which he has given us as the remedy for our sin. This sacrament teaches us to look to him, and not to ourselves. We see this in the story of Peter's denial and forgiveness.

* * *

When Jesus says at the Last Supper that all of his disciples will fall away from him that night, Peter protests: "Even if they all take offence at you, I will never take offence!" Peter apparently shares Jesus' poor opinion of the other disciples – but not of himself, of course. Jesus replies, "Amen, I say to you that this night, before the cock crows, you will deny me three times." But Peter protests again, "Even if I must die with you, I will never deny you!" (Mt 26:31ff).

But as we know, Peter does deny Jesus: "He denied it before them all, saying, 'I do not know what you are talking about'... And again he denied with an oath, 'I do not know the man'... Then he began to invoke a curse on himself and to swear, 'I do not know the man.' And at once the cock crowed" (26:69ff).

Anything that is said three times has a particular solemnity for the Bible. The angels in Isaiah's vision in the temple cry out, "Holy, holy, holy is the Lord of hosts!" (6:3), not because the threefold "holy" says anything more than the single affirmation "holy" would have said, but because the threefold affirmation expresses their deepest being as creatures who serve the holiness of God. Similarly, the sinful citizens of Jerusalem lull their consciences with "these deceptive words: 'This is the temple of the Lord, the temple of the Lord, the temple of the Lord'" (Jer 7:4), because they are so utterly sure that what counts is having the outer structure of worship, without any inner moral correspondence in their lives. The threefold acclamation expresses the depth of their unshakable sense of security, which makes them impervious to the prophecy that the Lord will let his temple be destroyed, "the house that is called by my name, in which you trust" (7:14). Examples in the New Testament narratives are Pilate's threefold acquittal of Jesus (cf. Lk 23:4,14,22) and the threefold account of Paul's conversion (cf. Acts 9,22,26), underlining the innocence of Jesus and the importance of Paul. We also have the threefold "Woe!" uttered at Rev 8:13, indicating the completeness of the devastation that will overtake "those who dwell on the earth".

When Peter denies Jesus three times, accordingly, this is more significant than one single denial, which might have been merely a momentary weakness. Peter solemnly asserts that he is not a disciple of Jesus. He twice takes an oath that this is the case. The threefold assertion indicates that Peter stands behind his words with the whole of his being: "I do not know the man". This is not a trivial sin, and it does not escape Jesus himself. Luke writes, "And all at once, while he was still speaking, a cock crowed. And the Lord turned round and looked at Peter, and Peter remembered the word of the Lord, when he had said to him, 'Before the cock crows today, you will deny me three times.' And he went outside and wept bitterly" (22:60ff). Once again, the encounter with Jesus – here, the encounter with his wordless look – reveals to Peter how sinful he is. And his reaction is to rush away and weep.

Through Peter's own initiative, the relationship between himself and Jesus has been broken: he is no longer one of the disciples (let alone their leader). For the relationship to be restored, it is Jesus who must take the initiative, just as he had taken the initiative in first calling Peter to follow him. And this is possible only *on the far side of the resurrection.* For (thanks in part to Peter's sins of cowardice and denial) Jesus has died before Peter could do anything to undo his solemn affirmations in the house of the high priest. Between Peter's sin and Peter's forgiveness lies the gulf of Jesus' death and resurrection.

The appendix to John's Gospel (21:15ff) tells how the risen Jesus solemnly forgives Peter, underlining the threefold confession of love with which Peter undoes his three-fold denial of Jesus. There are no reproaches on Jesus' part. He only asks one question: "Do you love me?" When he asks this a third time, Simon Peter is saddened and protests a little, "Lord, you know everything – you know that I love you!" Jesus might very well have replied that, after the scene in the high priest's house, he knew nothing of the sort. But he only replies, "Feed my sheep." For his forgiveness of Peter is expressed in a threefold call, a threefold commission: "Feed my lambs... be the shepherd of my sheep... feed my sheep." And then Jesus says, "Amen, amen, I say to you: when you were younger, you bound your girdle on yourself and went where you wished. But when you are old, you will stretch out your hands, and another will bind you and take you where you do not wish." The evangelist comments, "He said this to indicate by what kind of death Peter was to glorify God; and after saying this, he said to him, 'Follow me!'"

It is important to note that Jesus' act of forgiveness does not merely restore the status quo. He takes Peter more deeply into his vocation of configuration to Christ: he is to be a shepherd, just as Jesus himself is "the good shepherd" (10:11), and he is to "glorify God" by dying, just as Jesus "glorified" God by dying on a Cross (cf. 13:31 – there may very well be an allusion here to Peter's own death on a cross). This is what it means for him to "follow me". And lest we should overlook the point that it is a sinner and a coward who is given this charge, the evangelist continues by speaking of the one male disciple who had not failed when all the others fled, but had stood under the Cross and had received the mother of Jesus as his own mother: "Seeing this man, therefore, Peter said to Jesus, 'Lord, what about this man?' Jesus said to him, 'If I wish him to remain until I come, what is that to you? As for you, follow me!'" It is expressly stated that the chief pastoral ministry is given to the unfaithful Peter, not to this faithful disciple. Jesus' act of forgiveness is a renewed and deepened call to him to become more fully configured to his Lord, by sharing both in his ministry and in his dying.

* * *

What is the lesson for us, who recognise ourselves in the unfaithful Peter, rather than in the faithful disciple? The lesson, once again, is that his history can become "my history". When I realise my sinfulness and confess to the Lord my failure to love him, his act of forgiveness does not merely wipe the slate clean. His forgiveness is a fresh call to "follow", to "be the shepherd of my sheep", in a life that gives "glory" to God by its configuration to the logic of

Jesus' own self-giving. Absolution, therefore, is a new vocation, a new creation in my life. Through the priest, Jesus asks me, "Do you love me?" And if I say "yes" like Peter, all the rest of the dialogue in John 21 becomes a dialogue between the Lord and myself. I may, thanks to his grace, not have denied him in such a dramatic and public fashion as Simon Peter in the house of the high priest. But even if I should have done so, the story of Peter shows (to borrow Paul's words) that "where sin grew greater, grace abounded all the more exuberantly" (Rom 5:20). And the new creation of the Lord's forgiveness of my sin has the character of the "new heavens and new earth in which righteousness has its home" (2 Pet 3:13).

But there is nothing magic or automatic about this new creation and new vocation in the forgiveness of our sins. We always remain liable to fall back, and thus we always remain persons who need to confess our sins and be forgiven afresh. This too is seen in the story of St Peter, who (according to chapter 35 of the late-second-century Acts of Peter) escaped in disguise from Nero's persecution of the Christians in Rome. But as he was leaving the city, "he saw the Lord entering Rome. And when he saw him, he said, 'Lord, where are you going?' And the Lord said to him, 'I am going into Rome to be crucified.' And Peter said to him, 'Lord, are you to be crucified again?' He said to him, 'Yes, Peter, I am to be crucified again.'" Peter comes to himself and returns to Rome, where he is crucified head-downwards. We may leave aside the question of the historical accuracy of this *Quo vadis?* story; my point in quoting it (as with the references earlier to Medjugorje and the Italian book about Mary's life in Nazareth) is that it provides us with a wonderfully clear *image* that we can apply to our own lives. It shows that just as the initial call of Peter was not a once-and-for-all event, neither was the renewed call after the resurrection something that *guaranteed* that Peter would be absolutely faithful in the future. It remained possible for him to deny the Lord anew, and when he did so, it was once again the encounter with Jesus that brought him back to his true vocation.

Neither in John 21 nor in the Acts of Peter does Jesus utter a single word of reproach. Words of reproach are superfluous, because Peter recognises his own failure to love. All that is necessary is the renewed call to follow him, either explicitly as in John's Gospel or implicitly as in the Acts of Peter.

When we come to confession, Jesus does not reproach us for having sinned (and this is the theological reason why priests are not supposed to reproach penitents either). It is not that he dismisses our sins with an airy wave of the hand: he more than anyone knows the full seriousness of human sin, for he died because of the sins I am now confessing in the sacrament. But he knows that, if I myself did not recognise my failure to love, I should not be confessing it. And hence he can move on to what is more important: his own gift of a renewed call in the act of absolution. And he knows that if I should fall again, or even fall into worse sin, his grace will always be stronger.

The struggle within my heart between grace and sin will last as long as I live. But it is not an equal struggle – that idea is Manichaean, not Christian! We are always free to reject the love God offers us. But if we are even minimally open to it, it shows itself in the long run to be stronger than all our resistance and all our sins. We must never let the awareness of our sin frighten us away from saying and saying anew our "yes" to the Lord who calls us to consecrate our lives to him. *Of course* we are unworthy to serve him, *of course* we are unworthy to teach others the path of life. But let us stop looking at ourselves! Let us look instead at the one who knows us far better than we know ourselves, to the one from whom we can hide nothing of our sinfulness, but who nevertheless says to us, "Follow me." If *he* is calling us, that ought to end the discussion, because God does not make any mistakes. He knows what he is doing!

Let me repeat (since I am very liable to be misunderstood) that we must take our sin seriously. But let me repeat even more loudly that we must take the Lord's powerful grace more seriously still. The proper way to take temptations and sins seriously is to bring them to confession and throw them "like a great millstone into the sea". This image comes from the account of the destruction of Babylon, the city that was utterly hostile to God and therefore perished utterly (cf. Rev 18:21). But we discover the paradox that this sea is the sea of God's mercy: "He will again have compassion upon us," says Micah, "he will tread our iniquities under foot. You will cast all our sins into the depths of the sea" (7:19). Should we sin again, we must bring our millstone once again to the sea of God's illimitable mercy. The sacrament of penance allows us to experience the voice of Jesus inviting us to consecrate ourselves anew to his love, and this is why we shall never reach a stage here on earth at which we shall have left this sacrament behind us. For confession is the sacrament of hope.

XIV
Conclusion

Every vocation is an individual story, since God never repeats himself in exactly the same way. But since all Christian vocations take the form of following Jesus of Nazareth, and all the vocations of the Old Testament are in some fashion a preparation for his coming, there is a "family likeness" shared by all the individual stories. This means that we can learn to discern the patterns of our own story by meditating on the stories of others, and this has been the aim of the reflections in this book.

Discerning patterns is vitally important, precisely because each story is unique: the person called needs to have some idea of the basic biblical patterns, in order to get a perspective on the problems and questions that inevitably arise along the path. We must see how others have gone along what is fundamentally the same path. Then we can begin to see whether what is happening today in my particular story – something that perhaps seems very strange – is simply following a pattern staked out long ago.

In particular, I have had in mind the pervasive temptations to give up the path to which the Lord is calling me, when difficulties arise. If we see that these difficulties are normal, it becomes easier to hang on and to trust that we are being held in the hands of the Lord even when things look most negative and puzzling.

The style of this book has been very personal. I hope that it has not degenerated into a collection of reminiscences or anecdotes, but that the stories narrated have made the point of the first chapter: namely, that we ourselves are inescapably part of our testimony, and that it is in concrete human lives in time and space that the eternal

Word discloses himself and calls others to follow him. "He who is calling you is faithful," says St Paul (1 Thess 5:24). It is in the *narratives* of the Bible and of Christian history – and in the narratives of "my history" – that we see this divine faithfulness at work, and so learn to put our trust in the Lord. Only he deserves that kind of trust, and he deserves it richly and absolutely. As Moses says to Joshua (Deut 31:8), "It is the Lord who goes before you. He will be with you; he will not fail you or forsake you. Do not fear or be dismayed."

* * *

It is no doubt more customary to explain the dedication at the beginning of a book. If I have left this task until now, it is simply because readers tend to hop over such words in order to get on with the substance of the book. A relaxed coda at the end of the book may have a better chance of being read!

"His delight is in the law of the Lord," says Psalm 1:2. The dedication to the Revd Professor John O'Neill of Edinburgh University records my gratitude to a widely-read scholar, an extraordinarily gifted teacher and a good friend who has communicated to me over many years, not a mere detached academic knowledge of scripture, but a *glowing enthusiasm,* indeed a love, for the Word of God as something with power to transform human life. I hope I may have caught something of his "delight".

Playing God's Melodies
The psalms in our lives
by Jane Milward

Can the psalms help us to pray? Writing from her own experience, the author has no hesitation in recommending their use.

There is much richness, variety and beauty in the psalms. There is also much that responds to our longings and needs and, as they are part of Scripture, we believe that the Holy Spirit inspired their writers. From the time of King David, the psalms have been used by Jewish believers. Christians adopted them, and today continue to pray them.

In this book, the author tries to help in an opening out to God. She first considers Our Lady's *Magnificat*. There follow sections highlighting individual psalms and giving thoughts about interpretation, God, creation, Christ, sin, conversion and confidence leading on to thanksgiving and praise. The Conclusion gives some practical ideas for praying the psalms.

JANE MILWARD is a 'cradle Catholic' with a varied career, beginning in the Civil Service. Later she became a solicitor, obtaining Cambridge MA and LL M degrees. She worked in private practice, for a charity, and in publishing. She is now self-employed.

ST PAULS

Listening to silence

by Michel Hubaut

Silence, it would seem, is not much appreciated in today's world. Or it is held to be a luxury, though it is one we cannot do without, psychologically, spiritually, even physically. It is good to break away sometimes from the din, the tension and the rush of modern society and find peace and tranquillity in contemplating in silence. It is the purpose of this book to provide paths to this peace. The desert and solitude are the keynotes of the book but *Listening to Silence* shows the value of silence above all in the life of contemplative prayer in the heart. It is in praise of silence, not in psychological reference only but as leading to holy silence in the presence of God. There are two paths to silence, one solitude, the other, paradoxically, relationships, knowing when to be silent and when not. We need to find again the way to the heart by means of knowledge of God and of human beings through spiritual understanding and a new way of loving. Twofold also are the results of silence in outgoing to God and to others. Then, too, there is God's silence. Why does he not intervene?

This is not a theological treatise. It is intended only to help a person to faith.

MICHEL HUBAUT, a Franciscan, is a writer and retreat-giver and a contributor to several religious journals and reviews.

ST PAULS